THEISMANN

THEISMANN

BY JOE THEISMANN
WITH DAVE KINDRED

CONTEMPORARY
BOOKS, INC.
CHICAGO ▪ NEW YORK

Library of Congress Cataloging-in-Publication Data

Theismann, Joe.
  Theismann.

  1. Theismann, Joe.   2. Football players—United States
—Biography.   I. Kindred, Dave.
GV939.T44A3   1987   796.332′092′04 [B]   87-13907
ISBN 0-8092-4843-3

Published by Contemporary Books, Inc.
180 North Michigan Avenue, Chicago, Illinois 60601
Manufactured in the United States of America
International Standard Book Number: 0-8092-4843-3

Published simultaneously in Canada by Beaverbooks, Ltd.
195 Allstate Parkway, Valleywood Business Park
Markham, Ontario L3R 4T8 Canada

To my grandmother,
who always believed

Contents

Acknowledgments

Special thanks to my parents who gave when there was nothing to give; to my sister who grew up alone; to my children who were willing to share their father; to my coaches who saw potential in youthful enthusiasm; and to Cathy Lee, my teacher, friend, and lover. Because of them, there is this story to tell.

THEISMANN

Prologue

The boy had a dream and it was always the same. He wanted to be a pro quarterback like Bart Starr and Johnny Unitas. He took their pictures out of magazines and put them up on his bedroom wall, and he would study those pictures as if there were secrets to be learned from them.

The boy's bedroom was a place built in the attic by his father. If you weren't careful, you'd hit your head on the ceiling where it slanted down to a wall. The bedroom must have been tiny, scrunched under an eave that way, but in the boy's memory it was a grand place of imagination and hopes. Next to the pictures of Bart Starr and Johnny Unitas, the boy tacked up a copy of "The Champion's Creed." It began, "If you think you can, you will . . ."

Because he could throw better than most of his buddies, the boy was the shortstop in baseball games and the quarterback in football. He grew up in a New Jersey town of 10,000 people, an hour's drive from the big city. With his father, the boy would go to the bus station in their little town. They took the Port Authority bus into New York City. They hopped into the subway to Shea Stadium and got out behind the center-field wall. The boy stood under an open sky and looked up at how big the place was. Years later he would remember what he said the first time he saw it. He said, "Wow."

1
Bad Breaks

F alling to the ground under the weight of two or three New York Giants, I knew my leg was broken because the bones cracked with a sound like two gunshots. *Pow! Pow!*

The stadium crowd went silent. Players from both teams paced back and forth, not knowing what to do, just looking down at me lying on the 50-yard line. The only sound was my own voice.

"My leg is broken, my leg is broken. Please don't touch it," I told our trainer, Bubba Tyer. I asked our doctor, Charlie Jackson, "Did the bone come through?"

He said yes, the tibia had ripped the skin just above my right ankle on the inside of the leg. Blood soaked through my sock. And millions of football fans were watching this horrible scene, because it was a Monday night game, November 18, 1985. Though I didn't know it at the time and I would fight like hell to come back, I would never play another football game. And as much as breaking a leg hurts, it didn't hurt half as much as trying to accept the fact that the injury would change my life—and change it in ways I'm only beginning to understand.

You spend a lifetime getting to the National Football League. Then it's over as fast as two bones can be broken. Paul Newman as Fast Eddie in the old movie *The Hustler* tried to explain to his girlfriend why it was important for him to play pool again. He had his hands in casts after goons broke his thumbs as punishment for hustling them. He needed to play pool, Fast Eddie said, because that's when he felt the most alive, almost as if he were under a magical spell.

"The cue becomes part of me," Eddie said, "like it's connected to my nervous system, and I'm shootin' pool and I can't miss and it's so good, so really good."

Eddie without pool, Joe Theismann without football— suddenly, you feel less than you were. Not only are you less, you're someone you never wanted to be: you're a spectator. "Quarterback" was more than a job description; it was my life for 20 years, from South River (New Jersey) High School to Notre Dame, from Canada to the Redskins. There were sweet moments, when throwing the football was all magic, all so good, so really good.

I hasten to add that in 1985 there was a distinct lack of magic in my quarterbacking. In the nine games leading up to the broken leg, I was no better than mediocre. I threw five interceptions in our opener against the Cowboys. For reasons I never figured out, my confidence was shot and my concentration was terrible.

And that's the good news. Along the way I was not a nice guy about it. You name the excuse, I used it. Everything was wrong. Everybody screwed up. The offensive line, the receivers, the coaches. Everybody except Joe Theismann. I was beyond failure. I was perfect. I had won everywhere, from the Jersey sandlots to the Golden Dome to the Super Bowl. I was Mr. Quarterback.

All you had to do was ask me. And I'd talk some more. "Joe Theismann has never had an unexpressed thought," one sportswriter has written. Occasionally, I made good sense; more often, I annoyed people with my naive eagerness to have them believe what I believed. Namely, Joe Theismann could be a winning quarterback in the National Football League. A dozen years in the NFL proved that I could win. Yet in 1985, I could do almost nothing right.

I went so far as to modify Joe Gibbs's offense to fit my whims. To understand how stupid that was, you have to know that Joe Gibbs's offense was sensational. But I resented it. I wanted to do things my way. I'd throw deep when the play was supposed to go short. I'd throw over the middle instead of outside. Nobody knew what I would do next or why. Let's say Joe Gibbs wanted to run a short-yardage pass to one sideline. You don't even look at receivers on the other side of the field; you went for the first down, that's all.

But I was so far away from the program that instead of just taking the first down to keep the drive going, I decided to throw deep for the touchdown. Everyone would be thinking the pass was going to the sideline, when, *bam*, Mr. Quarterback throws deep.

Of course, it wouldn't work. Joe would be there when I came off the field, and I'd say, "Well, I thought the deep man had a chance." The game is moving too fast for Joe to argue right there. But later, when he sat down to study and grade the films—film doesn't lie—Joe would want to know why in the world I threw so many passes poorly or to the wrong people.

I'd say, "You can't see the defender's hand in my face." Or, "The clown ran the wrong pass route." A thousand different excuses, excuses that never would have occurred to me in '79 and '80 when I was battling to get the job. When things are going good, you forget the price you paid to get good. You say: "I don't need this. We beat 'em, 40–7, and I threw five touchdown passes. No coach is going to sit down with me and tell me I made a mistake by taking a six-step drop instead of a five-step drop. You're wasting my time."

My performance fell off drastically in '85, and I can see why it did. As a group, the Redskin coaches who took us to

two Super Bowl games were the most intelligent, under-
standing, creative men I ever worked with. Without fail,
they gave me the best possible tools to use in each game. If
they said, "When Dan Hampton moves from this gap to
that gap, we'll run this play," I would run that play with
full faith that it was the perfect play.

But not in 1985. I began to question everything. It was
like, "I know my job, now I'm going to show everybody
how smart I am by doing *their* jobs, too." I thought it
would help the club.

One day, Mr. Quarterback was explaining something to
our offensive coach, Dan Henning. Picture an old Western
movie where this tough guy sits outside the saloon, his
chair propped back, hat down over his eyes, a little piece of
straw hanging out of his mouth. This is a guy who knows
his stuff, right? Dan knew the Redskin system better than a
rocket scientist knows a rocket. But Mr. Quarterback
wanted to add his two cents to a conversation Dan was
having with Art Monk. I said, "We oughta move Art over
here . . ."

Dan looked at me. Out of the side of his mouth, he said:
"Y'know, Joe, we've got plenty of coaches. What we need
are players."

As big a problem as I was in '85, the coaches would give
me the benefit of the doubt because I had always produced
for them. They'd say, "OK, just do it better next week."
They'd let it pass one more time.

Then there was Stanley to contend with. Stanley, that's
me. Everybody has two sides, as Dr. Jekyll taught Mr.
Hyde, one side normal and one side ugly. Our line coach,
Joe Bugel, who kept a light touch at practices, would holler
during one of my ugly phases, "Oh, come on, Stanley."
Anytime Joe saw a sulk coming, he'd yell out, "Oh,
Stannnnnley." Stanley's ugly head reared itself too often in
'85, and somebody should have slapped us both around.

But no one did.

Hey, I was Joe Theismann, All-Pro Quarterback. I met
President Ford and President Carter. I had dinner with

President and Mrs. Reagan. I made a movie with Burt Reynolds. Such a big shot didn't need coaches grading him anymore, did he? Who needs to stay inside a system when he's as good as this big shot? The offense was built for me and our great fullback, John Riggins. It was a ball-control offense sustained by quick passes and power running. I could run this offense in my sleep.

In pro sports, though, you go from the penthouse to the outhouse one step at a time. You forget what got you to a championship. You forget the dues you paid to get good. You get so cocky you think you can do the work in your sleep.

So I began the 1985 season by throwing five interceptions in a 44–14 loss to Dallas. This is not as bad as losing a nuclear war to the Russians, but it's close. I even remember the date of this one (September 9) because it was my birthday and as I sat on the bench at game's end, the Texas Stadium crowd of 60,000 delirious fans started singing "Happy Birthday" to me.

The second week, I didn't recognize two blitzes coming even when Houston brought eight guys to the line of scrimmage. If I didn't see those guys, at least I should have heard them breathing. If you miss one blitz a month, that's too many. Suddenly, I missed two in one game. What was wrong?

After three really good years, it was clear that I had lost something. Accuracy had been my forte as a passer. I never had the Terry Bradshaw gun or the Dan Fouts quick trigger. But I damn well could put the ball where I wanted it. We're not talking about a ball that hits somebody in the chest. We're talking three inches below the chin. We're talking a 25-yard throw as accurate as if you walked up to a guy and handed it to him right where he wanted it.

But in '85, my good passes were a little high, a little low, a little behind. My bad passes—I wanted to forget them they were so bad. When the media knocked me from here to Timbuktu, the coaches protected me by saying it wasn't all my fault. They'd talk about the patchwork offensive line and they'd say receivers ran wrong routes. Thing is, even if all that were true, it shouldn't have mattered. It never mattered before. Winners find ways to win, losers find excuses for losing.

The truth is, we did have problems at positions other than quarterback. Our offensive line became a patchwork because of injuries. Joe Jacoby was out, Russ Grimm was hurt for a while. Against the Cowboys, we started a rookie, Dan McQuaid, and asked him to do the impossible, which was to keep defensive end Jim Jeffcoat out of my face. Our regular offensive line did not start intact two games in a row until after my injury.

We had new receivers, too, who were just not adequate. The only receiver I trusted was Art Monk. Period. Bobby Beathard is a great general manager and judge of personnel, but when he traded with the Raiders to get Calvin Muhammad and Malcolm Barnwell, Bobby became a blushing member of the "Don't Try to Outsmart Al Davis Club."

Right after we signed one of those guys, I happened to be on a plane with Bobby. You'd have thought he was the cat that swallowed the canary. Boy, was he happy to get Muhammad and Barnwell. But what everyone in football should have learned by now is that Raiders owner Al Davis is a very intelligent football man. If Al Davis doesn't want a player, there's a good reason for it. It seems the reason in this case was that these guys just couldn't play football any more.

Barnwell wasn't as fast as they thought. Muhammad, who had talent, couldn't comprehend our offensive system. Two of the interceptions in the Dallas game came because they ran bad pass routes. And it wasn't even a question of running the wrong pattern. They'd run on the wrong side of a defensive back, letting the back see the whole field instead of making him turn his back to me. So all the cornerback had to do was follow the ball and make the interception. A little thing, but in the NFL, little things become big things. A receiver who isn't smart enough to

.turn a cornerback away from the play can make the whole team look terrible and a quarterback's life miserable.

Another factor in our struggle was John Riggins. In what turned out to be his last year, too, he wasn't as effective as he'd been in our Super Bowl seasons. It really takes the pressure off a quarterback to know he can turn around and hand the ball to a great back and say, "Here, bail me out of this jam." Sonny Jurgensen had Bobby Mitchell, Joe Namath had Emerson Boozer and Matt Snell, Lenny Dawson had Mike Garrett, Johnny Unitas had Alan Ameche. Bart Starr could hand it to Jim Taylor (with Paul Hornung in the bargain). Terry Bradshaw had to be good to win four Super Bowls, but he always had Franco Harris back there.

In '82 and '83 John Riggins was one of the best running backs in football. No one was more dominating. It was a travesty that John never made a Pro Bowl team. Good God, he ran for two million yards against defenses stacked to stop him. He never talked about not making the Pro Bowl, but I sensed that being overlooked really disappointed him, and justifiably so.

It happens to all the great teams, that point when they begin to lose the edge. It begins with a period of growing pains when they're trying to learn who's who. If they're good athletes, they build an environment in which they enjoy each other's company and win a lot of football games while having the time of their young lives. But after three years, let's say, maybe they get a little bored, a little fat, a little sassy. Maybe they get tired, too, because they've played four exhibition games, 16 regular-season games, three playoff games, maybe a Pro Bowl. Twenty-four football games from July to February. If you do that two or three years, you're punishing your body something awful. There's a physical erosion going on, in addition to the mental strain.

Then the front office people, whose job it is to spot that erosion and shore it up, start bringing in new players, players who change the personality of the team. You may be dropping a high-salaried veteran whose talent has diminished, but you're doing it at the cost of losing the intangibles he brings, the leadership and inspiration.

Pretty soon, even if you've only changed six or seven guys, you've got a different football team. Maybe a better team, maybe not.

Those first nine weeks of '85, I even dreaded the half-hour drive from home to Redskin Park. Every Monday through Thursday was hell because I didn't want to be there. Yet I didn't know where I wanted to be. Maybe I just wasn't any good anymore. Maybe. But I don't think that was it. I still had the physical tools. I was 36 years old, not young but not old. OK, Joe Theismann was no longer 185 pounds of whipcord and steel. But I could move around and my arm was as strong as ever.

Physically OK, but mentally unsure—that may have been the answer to the mystery of my performance in '85. My work as an announcer for ABC-TV on Super Bowl XIX after the '84 season gave me a taste of what life might be like after football. Every minute of the TV job was fun. There I was at the Super Bowl, with all the excitement of the spectacle but with none of the pressure of having to win a game.

This was appealing to a guy who had worked so hard for 20 years playing football. For the first time, this question came up: did I want to work all those hours on the practice field when I could just sit in a TV booth and do something I loved? The answer: maybe not.

Unfortunately, that attitude is not conducive to success. To play this game, a guy needs fire in his gut. You must want it more than anything. A football player must need football the way Fast Eddie needed pool to feel alive. For 20 years I needed the game enough to pay heavy-duty dues in training, practice, commitment, injuries, and criticism. But broadcasting for that Super Bowl changed something. It doesn't sound like much. It was like touching the corner of a portrait on the wall, raising it a quarter-inch. Now the picture looks different. The room looks different. *Some-*

thing has changed, but what?

I couldn't figure it out, but I knew this: you have to have a lot of little boy in you to play football. And the little boy was no longer running around inside me. He had disappeared, and I couldn't figure out how to get him back.

So I hoped, the way you do when you're groping, that the Monday night game with the Giants would get me excited. You can be dead and still get excited about a Monday night game.

I felt good going in—even though I had won money that afternoon from my card-playing buddy, tackle Mark May. During our good years I had developed the superstition that if I lost money at cards before a game, I'd go out and play great. Our defensive coordinator, Richie Petitbon, would always check with me. "How'd you do?" he would say.

"I got killed."

And he'd say, "Great. I feel better already."

It became a barometer. If I won at cards, I'd play lousy. And Richie would get all over Mark, saying, "May Day, you gotta beat him."

On that Monday before the Giants game, I won more money from May Day playing gin than ever before.

This was a big game because we were contending for a playoff spot. Of my first 10 passes, I completed seven. People later said I played with confidence, but appearances are deceiving. That night, like the whole year, was strange and scary. If you have to work at feeling confident, you always feel on the verge of losing control. It's like rocking back on a chair until you're balanced on the two back legs and you don't know if you're going to tip over.

The Giants sacked me two or three times when I scrambled out of the pocket and ran smack into somebody. Not a good sign, but I tried to ignore it. Every quarterback runs into some sacks. The difference was that I always had offset a negative play with a dozen positive plays. Not in '85.

In the second quarter we were moving the ball on the Giants. We called a trick play, the "throw-back special." The handoff goes to John Riggins, he moves into the line, he takes two steps, and pitches the ball back to me. It had worked for us in the past, even for touchdowns.

This time John tossed it to me, and I looked deep. But before I had a chance to see anything, the pocket started to cave in. Jim Burt was closing in. And Lawrence Taylor. And then it happened. I didn't see it, but I heard it, and certainly felt it.

The Giant linebackers, all great ones, had not been fooled by the handoff to Riggins. They penetrated in a hurry. Harry Carson almost had me, but his arm slipped off mine. Then there was pressure coming from the left. It was Taylor, who ran a big, sweeping route. Because of the pressure, I stepped to my right. It was too late to complete a pass, so I was going to throw the ball away.

Suddenly, Taylor grabbed me high and swung around with his right thigh, catching my right leg full force between ankle and knee.

Pow! Pow!

Jim Burt would say later, "Oh, God, it was awful. It sounded like two helmets banging together."

All I saw of the injury was one replay the next Thursday. It was awful. My leg snapped sideways like a toothpick. Believe me, I'll never watch it again.

Even as Dr. Jackson helped strap me on a stretcher, I thought, "It just can't end this way." I wanted something special. Maybe another Super Bowl ring. Some good work to set everything right again. Instead, it ended with a broken leg.

On the field, I looked up at Harry Carson, one of those Giant linebackers who make a quarterback's life miserable. "Harry, don't you go and retire. I'm going to be back," I said.

Harry said, "Yeah, but not tonight, Joe."

As they rolled me across the field on a stretcher, I looked up at the night sky. RFK's lights made a circle against the darkness. It was eerie. It was like I was floating out of there on a soft wave of sound. Everyone was applauding. No shouting, no whistling, just 55,000 people clapping, just applauding for a guy who'd been hurt. Maybe they knew I'd never be back.

"A heckuva mess you've left us in," Joe Gibbs said gently to me on my way off the field, and then from the light and noise they rolled me into a dark, silent tunnel on the way out of the stadium.

As I reached the end of the tunnel, there came a tremendous roar from inside the stadium. The last Redskin I had seen was Jay Schroeder. I had told him, "You get the job done, Jay. I know you can do it." What I didn't know was that Jay would do it so damned fast. That roar came up because Jay had thrown a long pass to Art Monk down the sidelines, exactly the kind of pass we hadn't hit all season. Without me, the Redskins had scored in about a minute.

Fame is fleeting, but this was ridiculous. I wasn't even in the ambulance yet. But old warhorses die hard. Sonny Jurgensen didn't like it when Billy Kilmer took his job. Billy Kilmer didn't like it when Joe Theismann took his job. Joe Theismann didn't like it when . . .

Well, it was nothing personal. I didn't want Jay to break a leg. It wouldn't have bothered me all that much, though, if he just threw a wobbly pass once in a while.

While I was being wheeled through the tunnel, Ted Koppel and a couple of security guards were rushing Cathy Lee from her seat in Jack Kent Cooke's box to the tunnel entrance. We arrived there about the same time, she grabbed my hand, and the tears rolled down my face. I said, "I guess this is the end of my punting career." (For those who may not know, and for those Redskin fans who choose not to remember, I should explain that I had the distinction of punting a ball one yard against the Bears seven weeks earlier. It probably didn't seem like the right time for humor, but I was really searching for something.)

Cathy Lee rode with me in the ambulance to the hospital. She kept asking if my leg was hurting. The pain had stopped and I had this total numbness from my knee to my toes. I kept looking at my leg, hoping that what had happened was just a bad dream.

At the hospital, I watched the game's last four minutes outside the operating room on a little black-and-white TV they hooked up with a coat hanger for an antenna. With about a minute left in the game, the Redskins, who were winning, moved the ball to midfield. Then the doctors wheeled me into surgery and started the anesthetic.

Because the injury happened on national TV, everyone saw it, and the next morning the media blitz began. I had never been averse to media blitzes, witness a few million pages of notebooks and a few thousand hours of recording tape filled with my words in interviews from coast to coast from dawn to dusk. But I was not eager to turn a broken leg into a media event.

"Good Morning America," "CBS Morning News," "Today," *Sports Illustrated, The Washington Post,* and *The New York Times* all wanted to interview me in the hospital. That was normal, under the circumstances. The unusual part was that I didn't want to talk to them. I just wanted some time to think about things.

Cathy Lee and I did go on "Monday Night Football" at halftime the next week to thank the thousands of wonderful people who sent the letters, telegrams, cards, and flowers. It was unbelievable.

And then came the experts. They trotted out diagrams, charts, diagnoses, and prognoses. Everyone had an idea of what Joe Theismann could and couldn't do.

Because I *knew* I would play football again, these so-called experts irritated me. One actually had a skeleton on TV. The guy took a hammer and said, "This is what happened to Joe Theismann." He meant to crack the leg. But the skeleton wasn't tied down, and when he whacked at it, the whole thing went flying across the room like it was some comedy bit.

Trust me, there's nothing funny about a broken leg. You could ask Lawrence Taylor. When he realized what he'd done, he became hysterical, like he was about to cry. He slapped his hands against his helmet in shock or horror. I felt sorry for him. He had no intention of hurting me. He hit me high and then fell on my leg.

"It went through me," Lawrence told reporters later. "I felt like it happened to me. It made me sick."

Watching the film later, I said, "Lawrence may never be the same after this." Happily, I was wrong about that. After putting himself through a drug rehabilitation program and after the experience with my bloody leg, Lawrence came back in 1986 to have his best year and to help the Giants win their first Super Bowl. Good for him.

Lawrence called me in the hospital that first week and asked how I was. "You broke both bones in the leg," I said, and L.T. said, "Joe, you know, I just don't do things halfway. Get well quick."

In 1985, my year of living dumb, I'd forgotten the basic truths of football. It's fun. It's a team thing. It's a *game*. Somehow, football for me had become a show, a Roman circus. I'd think: "We're gladiators here to die for you. You, the fans, don't care about us, you're only here to turn thumbs down or thumbs up. I'll do my job, take the money, and get out of here." I had loved everything about football: how the ball felt . . . the smell of the grass . . . the chess game of move and countermove a quarterback plays with a defense . . . the dependency on your teammates . . . the thrill that comes when a team of 45 men succeeds as one.

Always an overachiever, a skinny little runt who worked hard because he loved to play, I betrayed all that in 1985. Suddenly I was out there simply to do my job and earn my money.

It took the broken leg to straighten me out. Tens of thousands of letters came from people from all over the country. The Dallas Cowboys' secondary sent flowers with a note: "Hurry back soon, we miss you." A fan in Dallas wrote, "Dear Joe, Please get well soon so we can BOOOOOO you some more."

To lighten things up, I asked permission from the hospital to keep at my bedside a double-barreled, sawed-off . . . rubber-dart gun. This was at the height of our team's comic-relief game of "Assassin." You know, you "shoot" a guy when his guard is down, and the last one to survive wins. Well, ruthless people that my teammates were, I figured one would sneak into my room and "off" me. This was serious stuff. In both my restaurants, I sat with my back to the wall in a spot where I could see the front door and the kitchen door. Guys from Jersey know about this kind of stuff, but a kid from California, like Charles Mann, was so innocent that he was wasted during the first night of the team's Bible study. Rich Milot, our answer to Rambo, liked to ring doorbells, jump back in the bushes, and wait for the victim to open up. But the guys caught on to that scheme quickly. They sent their wives to answer the door.

Armed and dangerous, if a little slow afoot, I spent a week in the hospital, and Cathy Lee never left my side. And there are two other things I'll never forget about being there: Jack Kent Cooke came to see me, Joe Gibbs didn't.

Mr. Cooke owns the Redskins, the Chrysler Building, the *Los Angeles Daily News*, Elmendorf Farm in Kentucky, a $755 million cable-TV company, and most anything else he wants to own. Mr. Cooke is an incredibly busy man. But Mr. Cooke came by the hospital. We talked about everything from football to real estate. It was a great visit that left me feeling positive and encouraged about returning to the Skins.

Some teammates stopped by. Mark May, one of my closest friends, had no mercy for a man with a broken leg. As usual, May Day beat me at gin and took my money. Jeff Bostic stopped in. So did Clint Didier, Jay Schroeder, Mark Moseley, and a few others. Not a big turnout from 45 guys, right? OK. You learn.

When I asked Joe Gibbs why he never came by, he said he had been busy that week getting ready for the next game.

I said, "OK, but what about the night it happened?"

He said, "I was tired." Yeah. Right. I was a little tired myself that night.

"You could have stopped by sometime," I said. "You talk about how much I meant to this football team and you give me all your bullshit about caring about people, but when it comes down to brass tacks, you don't even stop by."

Joe said, "I'm really sorry."

He had lost touch with reality. Joe Gibbs was so caught up in his insulated world of football that nothing else mattered. I was no longer important to him because he had to get ready for the next game. John Madden drove 120 miles every day for months to visit Darryl Stingley in the hospital after Stingley was paralyzed—and Stingley wasn't even on Madden's team. Joe Gibbs didn't drive downtown to see me.

Five weeks after breaking my leg, five weeks of hobbling around on crutches, five weeks of having my mother take care of this whimpering invalid—after five weeks of misery, I asked Joe if I could come to the last home game and stand on the sidelines with the team. This seemed routine enough. Joe's answer was anything but routine.

He said no.

To understand how much that hurt, you have to know how much the five weeks out had changed my attitude about the game. The fire in my gut had flamed up again. I wanted to set everything right, to show that the game was the most important thing in my life and always would be. Now that I couldn't play, I wanted to play more than ever.

It was hell watching the Redskins on TV those five weeks. When you've been part of a team for 12 years and suddenly you're out of the picture, you feel disoriented. There's no anchor to your life. No locker room to go to. You don't smell the same aromas any more. Where's the liniment? The dirty socks? The distinctive sweatshop ambience? When they cut you off from your life's senses, so highly developed over all those years, you can have odd, even contradictory thoughts. After all the years of wanting to win, now you might want your team to lose. You want them to miss you. And if they lose, they'll know how important you were.

Childish. But you think it.

Listen, I will be a Redskin fan forever, but that was my

job on the line out there when Jay Schroeder took over. If
the kid did well, it's see ya later, Joe. I could have walked up
to Jay in the locker room and said: "Look, you did a
helluva job, but I gotta be honest. I sat home and hoped you
didn't play well. Don't get hurt, but don't do real good."

It's the nature of the competitive beast. Sonny Jurgensen
wasn't ready to hand over the job to Billy Kilmer. Billy
wasn't ready to hand it to me. Nobody is ever ready to give
his job to some kid and hope he makes All-Pro and wins
every week. If you're willing to just walk away, you're no
kind of fighter and you're no kind of football player. Jay
will be a very good quarterback. He's got the job now, but
someone, someday, will take it away from him. And I
guarantee he won't like it, either.

At Jay's first game as my successor, someone put up a
gigantic sign: "SCHROEDER'S RAIDERS." Nice. The
night my leg was broken, someone had hung a banner that
said, "THEISMANN'S OVER THE HILL—HE
SHOULD GIVE IT UP."

Those signs were proof of the truth in the cliché:
"You're only as good as your last game."

Every game for 12 years, I was on the Redskin sidelines,
whether holding the clipboard for George Allen or running out to beat the Cowboys for Joe Gibbs. Broken leg and
all, I wanted to be there for the last home game of '85. So I
met with Gibbs in the middle of the last week.

"I thought about coming to the game the week after I got
hurt," I said.

Joe was surprised. He said he was glad I didn't do that
because my presence would have been disruptive. That
should have been a signal that Joe didn't want me around
at all, but I asked the question anyway.

"What about me coming to the Cincinnati game, the last
home game?"

Whenever Joe Gibbs was hesitant to say what he thought,
he stammered out parts of sentences, leaving it up to you to
figure out what he meant. This time, after fumbling

around, he said, "I think it would be better if you didn't come, Joe."

"Why?"

"I think it may have an effect on the team," he said.

Not a word out of me.

Joe went on. "It may, you know, I think, maybe, er, uh, take away the intensity of the game and put pressure on our team."

So I didn't go to the last home game of the last season in my 12 years as a Washington Redskin, because the coach considered me a distraction. I couldn't understand it. When Jim Plunkett was hurt, he stood with the Raiders. Steve Grogan broke his leg and he stood on the side with the Patriots. I wanted to be there with my teammates.

But damned if I would ask a second time. I'd been Joe Gibbs's quarterback for six years. Should I have to beg to go to a stinking game? I wanted to wave to the people and thank them for caring. I wanted to be loyal to my teammates who had helped me so much. In 12 seasons, I had earned the right to be there.

Instead, I stayed home and watched the game on TV. For a while Cincinnati was winning, and it was a nice game to see. Then the Redskins made a comeback. The stronger they looked, the less I liked it. So I turned off the TV because on that day, under those circumstances, I didn't want to see Joe Gibbs win.

My leg was in a cast. There was doubt I'd ever play again, and a coach who had been close to me suddenly didn't want me around. I was confused, angry, and, most of all, hurt. Such odd thoughts: you're no longer a Redskin, so you want them to lose; you want the kid to fall flat on his hind end; you want them to feel bad, too. You're in a cast, you can't even take a shower, you're feeling dirty and grungy, you can't walk to the kitchen sink to get a glass of water because you can't carry it hobbling on crutches. You feel like a fool. And if you're watching the Redskins play and they're winning without you, you might not like it. You might hear the announcers talking about how good this kid Schroeder looks. You might turn off the TV.

In January, Joe Gibbs asked me to come see him at Redskin Park. If events weren't unpleasant enough toward the end of the season, the toughest lesson was yet to come.

Joe said, "Would you be satisfied to be the No. 2 quarterback? If not, would you consider retiring?"

He knew the answers. My publicly outlined plan was to come back stronger than ever. I blew up.

"Damned if I'll quit," I said. "And would you want me on this team if I was willing to be No. 2? C'mon Joe, I couldn't live with myself if I said that. How can you ask that? I refuse to be associated with somebody willing to settle for No. 2 without even trying. You weren't satisfied as an assistant coach. Now you're asking me if I'd accept being No. 2?"

Joe couldn't bring himself to say the hard stuff he wanted to say. It was as if he wanted me to take the burden off him. He wanted me to retire so he wouldn't have to make a decision to cut me. No deal. While we agreed on how badly I'd played in '85, we disagreed on the remedy. He wanted me gone; I wanted a comeback.

There was no way after 12 years that I would just hand the job to somebody. It was mine. I earned it and I loved it. No, I couldn't be satisfied being No. 2. I also wasn't willing to retire.

So I wanted to keep my job a little longer. How much longer? Approximately forever.

2
So Much for the Wild Side

Toby Theismann didn't want her scrawny beanpole of a son to play football. She was petrified I'd get hurt. But the Pop Warner League coach, Ray Mazurowski, kept coming by the house to tell Mom not to worry. He got her to go to practice once, which wasn't such a hot idea because Mom saw the tackling and she said, "Such little boys, and they really *mean* it."

Until I was 12, I only played basketball and baseball. I loved baseball. I was a shortstop who could cover ground and throw. Even through college I played baseball, but I never was a big enough hitter to have pro potential. After Coach Mazurowski and I wore down my mother's defense, football became the passion in my life.

My whole world was sports. Even if I had a date, it meant going to a basketball game because I dated a cheerleader. Homework came behind sports and girls, so I made mostly C's and D's with A's in shop and phys ed.

This was in the mid-1960s, when everyone was a rebel, and why not? We had the Beatles changing music, Vietnam

changing politics, LSD changing our minds. We had
Muhammad Ali talking us into a frenzy and we had Joe
Namath taking girls up to his apartment to show them his
llama-skin rug. I didn't know it, but the Sexual Revolution
was under way. Me, I was a nerd looking to play catch.
You're talking to a guy who set records for being square.

I wanted to be a hood. Yeah, walk on the wild side. I
wanted to be with the tough guys at the Colonial Diner in
South River. We'd shoot some pool, smoke some cigarettes.
We'd wear our black leather jackets, yeah. Roll a pack of
cigarettes up in the sleeve of my black T-shirt, slap some
grease on my ducktail—let's rumble. I wanted to do it. I
wanted to revolt against the establishment. And I would
have, except for one thing.

I thought, "God, if I get caught, they'll kick me off the
football team." That, and my Dad would kill me. I mostly
went to the pizza parlor. So much for the wild side.

The South River, New Jersey, of my boyhood memory
was a rural town of about 10,000 people with maybe 1,000
kids in South River High. We were an hour's drive from
New York City. South River was an immigrant's town, with
an ethnic mix of Slavs, Poles, Germans, Hungarians, and
blacks.

Like the town and our neighborhood, my parents are an
ethnic mix. Mom is of Hungarian descent, and Dad's
father, Joseph Theismann, came over from Austria as a boy
with his father. My grandfather was the first Joe Theismann. Dad is the second. I'm the third and my son is the
fourth. In 1910, the farmer John Theismann left Blid,
Austria, near the Hungarian border. He entered this country at Ellis Island, where, my grandfather Joseph says, he
announced to immigration officials, "My name is John
Theismann," the last name pronounced *Thizemon.* He
settled in Bucks County, Pennsylvania. That's wonderful
farming country, and there he taught his sons the value of
working hard.

What he did is probably a crime nowadays, but back
then it was a matter of survival for those people brave

enough to start a new life in a world where they didn't speak the language. He leased out his sons to work for other farmers.

I say "leased out." They said, "We're selling the boys for a year." They were sent off to farms as far as 20 miles from home to work for a year, sometimes longer, and my great-grandfather John would be paid $30 each for them. He needed the money to run his farm and provide for his wife.

Later, my grandfather Joseph had his own farm in Pennsylvania until he and his wife, Eva, moved to New Brunswick, New Jersey. He worked there 41 years for Paulus Dairy. My father was born in 1923, my mother in 1925. They both grew up in New Brunswick but only met on a blind date less than a year before Dad was drafted into World War II.

Dad loves to tell how he won Mom's heart. . . .

"A guy who worked for me at the gas station asked me to go on a double date with him. It was wintertime, and we were headed for Asbury Park, New Jersey, to go swimming in one of those indoor pools they had. The guy said to me, 'I got two girls for us.'

"We picked up the first one and she sat in the car beside me. For my buddy's date, we had to stop for a girl named Toby. Her real name was Olga Tobias. So we pulled up at the door to pick up this second girl. Blind dates, they ain't always what they're cracked up to be. But we pulled up to the house and I saw Toby standing there. I changed my mind right then about blind dates.

"I said to myself, 'Out of the two, I'll take this Toby one.' I passed the other girl to the guy working for me, and I set Toby down with me in the back seat. Everybody was real upset for a while, but nobody dared say anything to the boss. We went on from there."

The month before Joseph John Theismann went into the Army, he married Olga Tobias, also a child of immigrants. They were married on November 29, 1942. He was 19, she 17. Love, if it's real, is forever. It's real for these two, and right now they're probably off on a golf trip together. Everyone should be so happy.

Happiness was always part of our family. With both Mom and Dad working, they made about $12,000 a year, not much money even in a lower-middle-class town. Dad ran a liquor store 13 hours a day, six days a week. That was soft after his first job, 100 hours a week at "Theismann's Esso." His gas station went out of business when they built an overpass on the spot where the station stood. Mom worked as a proofreader at the national headquarters of the Boy Scouts of America. The Boys Scouts are now located in Dallas of all places.

My parents never said no. Maybe because I was Mom's "million-dollar baby." She called me that because it was seven years into her marriage before I came along. She wanted a baby, but something wasn't working right. So Mom and Dad went to a hot-shot doctor in New York City. His prescription was, "Take her home and get her drunk."

After all those years of trying, I wonder if she sometimes looks at me and asks herself if I turned out the way she wanted.

Four years after I was born, my sister Patty came along. She had red hair and I teased her unmercifully. I'd call her all those names redheads have to go through life hearing, "Carrot Top," and "Fire Brain" to name two.

Through our years in South River, my sister Patty suffered because everyone knew her only as "Joey Theismann's little sister." I feel bad about that now, but I was so busy playing ball as a kid that I didn't even recognize that there was a problem, and we never shared much. Today, we're very close.

Dad had been a sandlot baseball player and amateur boxer as a kid. He loved football, too, so on Sundays we'd drive into New York City to see the Jets or Giants. As tired as he was from working, I'd wake him up out of his chair and say, "C'mon, Dad, let's go throw the football around." He never said no. He always had time for his kids.

My parents were always there for me, and that's something you appreciate only later in life when you find out what being a parent really means. They taught me love, and they taught me to work hard and to respect discipline even in things as small as going to bed.

Bedtime was 10 o'clock at the Theismann house, but I would sneak partway down the stairs and sit there peeking through the bannister to watch TV over Dad's head. At 10:30, never looking back, he would say, "I think you've watched it long enough, Joey. Go to bed now." To this day, I wonder how the heck he knew I was up there?

I was six weeks old when we moved into Grandma Tobias's house. Mom's father had died and we went to live with Grandma in the house she had lived in for 52 years. With Mom and Dad working, my grandmother spent more time raising Patty and me than they could.

Mom would be worn out from working all day. Then she would come home and make dinner for Dad, Patty, and Grandma at 5:15 on the dot. I'd be playing ball and might not get home until after dark. Mom had to rewarm the food, and she'd still be washing pots and pans at 10 o'clock.

Sometimes she'd get mad, and you couldn't blame her. She was always driving me to practices and waiting supper. But Grandma would tell her not to get upset. She'd say, "Mark my words, someday you're going to see that boy on television." That may have come true, but when I was growing up, I never really appreciated all the sacrifices my Mom made for me.

Time magazine did a cover story in 1985 about the Baby Boom generation, the 76 million of us born between 1946 and 1964. Reggie Jackson is in there and if you blur it a year or two, you get Muhammad Ali and Joe Namath. *Time* said: "The Baby Boomers were the Spock generation, the Now generation, the Woodstock generation. Nor were they exactly shy about all the attention. Through high times and hard times, no other group of Americans has ever been quite so noisily self-conscious."

The story talked about "generational arrogance" and the Baby Boomers' need for instant gratification and how they "avoided or postponed commitment to others." We wanted the important job, the fancy car, the jewelry and furs. The Baby Boomers wanted it all. As Muhammad Ali said in his shortest poem, "Me, Whee!"

Me? You bet. At quarterback for the Baby Boomers, No. 7 in your program, No. 1 in his mind, Joe Theismann!

As wonderful as my parents were about nonmaterialistic things, I became very materialistic. There was a "mansion" on Main Street in South River. Jeff Burns lived there. I wanted to be friends with this guy because he had money, a big house, a swimming pool, and a good-looking sister. I wanted that big house to be my house. I'd dream about walking around in my big house, throwing a party for all my friends. And I *hated* parties.

But I was 17. What did I know?

I knew this: it would be great to get that big house by becoming a pro football player. I was obsessed with the idea. I read that a quarterback's passes had to have "good touch." I wasn't sure what "good touch" was, but I set up garbage cans across the yard and threw footballs the 30 yards into them to practice "good touch."

In 1965, my junior year in high school, Joe Namath came to the Jets. They gave Alabama Joe a contract worth $427,000. I thought: "Hot ticket. This is it." All through high school, I wore high-top black football shoes because of Y.A. Tittle and Johnny Unitas. After Namath arrived, I said, "Give me a white pair like Joe Willie's."

To see the Jets play, Dad and I would take the bus into the Port Authority and ride the subway to the ballpark. Wow. I ate hot dogs and never took my eyes off Joe Namath. I watched him warm up. I watched him throw. I thought: "God, look at the way he throws. I would love to throw that way someday."

And it wasn't just football. He had it all. There was the image, the hot-shot bachelor guy. What a life. All the girls you want. Touchdown passes. Money. The apartment. The llama-skin rug. Joe Namath had a llama-skin rug. Me, Whee!

Well, I didn't know a llama from a camel from a yak, but I knew that my hero had a llama-skin rug. So give me Jeff Burns's house, give me $427,000, give me a few hundred TD passes. What more could a human being want?

Hey, I was 17. My problem was, I still thought that way at 34.

But the thing is, you're in no hurry to grow up if you're having fun as a kid—and nobody ever had more fun at football than I.

Soon it was time to choose a college, the first big decision of my football life. I had wanted to go to Duke. I had seen Duke on TV. They had great-looking uniforms, blue and white with nice blue letters. Really neat. And my eyes were blue. So that made sense to a kid of 17. Yeah, I'd go to Duke.

Then one day it dawned on me that you probably shouldn't choose a college because you like the color of its football uniforms, not to mention that academically I couldn't even get in. Another idea came to me: my high school coach, Ron Wojicki, had played behind Roman Gabriel at North Carolina State. Then Gabriel went on to be quarterback for the Los Angeles Rams, and I thought: "My coach played with Roman Gabriel. State's the place for me."

As soon as I signed a grant-in-aid to attend North Carolina State, though, the recruiting picture changed. I had visited North Carolina, Wake Forest, Penn State, and Notre Dame, along with N.C. State. A lot of schools wanted me. But when I said, "N.C. State," everybody's attitude changed. One minute I'm the greatest thing since sliced bread, the next minute I'm a moldy piece that didn't belong in the loaf.

So the ego trip of recruiting came to a screeching halt. That forced me to think about what I really wanted. Did I want Duke's pretty white uniforms with blue letters? Suddenly the Roman Gabriel-N.C. State connection didn't seem important, either. I used to tell people I wanted to go to State because I was going to study nuclear engineering—

they had a nuclear reactor on campus. I wanted people to think I was smart. But all I really wanted was to play football.

Then I got a second call from Notre Dame, asking me to make another visit. Until my senior year at South River, I knew nothing about Notre Dame. I never saw Notre Dame football on TV. I didn't know who Knute Rockne was. I'd never heard about George Gipp or shaking down thunder from the sky. I was 17 and too busy playing ball to know much else. (I wasn't even Catholic; I'm Methodist.)

In the Notre Dame recruiting process, they'd have prospects play basketball. All the football coaches would be there to watch you, supposedly just to be hospitable but really to check out your total athletic ability. Basketball tells a lot about your strength, quickness, lateral movements, eye-hand coordination. So I went through this test on my second trip there. And to this day, I don't know what they saw.

It was a gloomy, overcast, typical South Bend day. But something clicked for me on that visit. On the plane home, I knew Notre Dame was it. I told my parents I had changed my mind. There was no other place for me to go to school. Although my dad never tried to influence me, he had wanted me to go to Notre Dame from the start. Turns out one of us had heard about Knute Rockne and George Gipp.

3
Theesman, Thighsman, You Heard It Here

I had learned enough about the Notre Dame tradition and its place in football to know it was for me. If you want to be a doctor, go to Johns Hopkins. Go to Harvard, if law is it. I wanted pro football. For pro football, Notre Dame was the place. It was my Harvard.

Just in case they had recruited some Methodist out of New Jersey, who had never heard of Notre Dame, my first week they showed us the movie *Knute Rockne, All-American.* It's the one with Ronald Reagan as George Gipp and Pat O'Brien as Rockne. Watching it, you get the idea that Notre Dame has all these ghosts helping it win every week.

Unfortunately, not everyone agreed that I was a legend-in-the-making. A Jersey newspaper headline read, "LITTLE JOE TO GET KILLED AT NOTRE DAME." And that paper was not alone in figuring I might be too small for Notre Dame. When I showed up at South Bend in 1967, two assistant coaches met the plane. The linebacker coach, John Ray, saw me first, all 148 pounds of me, and grabbed coach Joe Yonto's arm. "Who's that skinny kid?" Ray said, and Yonto said, "That's the quarterback I recruited."

"Oh, no," Ray said. "They're going to break his neck." (I certainly didn't think so. Sure, there were six other quarterbacks there, and all of them were 6'4", but I decided, the way dreamers do when they're scared to death, that I was going to be the best of the bunch and the best in Notre Dame history. So there.) Even Ara Parseghian had second thoughts. My first scrimmage as a freshman against the varsity put me against great players like Alan Page, Jim Lynch, and Kevin Hardy. Ara said: "They'd beat him into the ground, and I'd think that was the end of little Joe. But he always got up for more."

My sophomore year, 1968, I spent our first seven games sometimes returning punts, but mostly sitting on the bench behind Terry Hanratty, the 6'2", 210-pound Heisman Trophy candidate. I was 5'11", maybe 155, all arm, and candidate for nothing. Suddenly, all that changed. In the seventh game, Hanratty was injured. Coach Parseghian could have used Coley O'Brien, who'd been the quarterback the year before, but Ara took an enormous chance on a sophomore who'd played only a few minutes all season. Me.

When Coach Parseghian told me I would start, everything changed. I played the game in my mind the night before. I didn't sleep at all. And then it was game day, and then . . .

The morning of the game I'm walking through the woods around the lake by St. Joseph's monastery, where we stay the night before games. I'm too nervous to just sit in my room and wait. I'm walking and I'm thinking, "This is my first start." I'm scared and I'm praying, "Please God, if you got a minute this afternoon, check on me, will you?"

It's one thing to be on a team as a reserve and punt returner who knows he's not going to play much, if at all. You're relaxed because you have very limited responsibility. The game won't be won or lost on something you do. You look around the locker room and have fun.

It's another thing, a very different thing, to be making

your first quarterback appearance for Notre Dame.

Everybody in the locker room is looking at me, little Joey Theismann who's going to get killed, and if I go to the bathroom once, I go 15 times. Scared to death.

Look, two years before, I had never heard of Knute Rockne. Then all of a sudden I'm playing for the ghosts of Notre Dame. Johnny Lujack and Frank Leahy and Rockne and Gipp—they didn't know about me two years ago, but suddenly they're sitting on my shoulder whispering advice.

I look at my teammates around the locker room. Do they know how scared I am? I'm trying to put on this air of confidence like, hey, be cool, guys, everything's under control. Meanwhile, I'm heading back to the john.

Everybody's up for the game. Everybody's dressed. It's almost time to leave the locker room. There are occasional shouts and whoops and lockers clanging when somebody kicks a door. Then, in one voice, everybody's roaring. ROARRRRR! LET'S GO-OOOOOO!

I pull on my helmet, snap the chin strap, and we go from this bright, roaring locker room into a dark little stairway where you have to hold on to a railing to get down. It leads us to a dark passageway. We're somewhere under the stadium seats in this dark tunnel, and there's a chill in the air and a dank smell like an old basement.

We've stopped walking in the tunnel now and we're waiting to be introduced, and ahead of us you can see light streaming to the tunnel entrance. You hear the crowd sounds kind of muffled, like thunder far away, and you hear the Notre Dame fight song. They're introducing our guys one at a time. For each one there's a *ROAR!* For their guys, a *BOOOO!*

Then it's my turn to go out. I run out there and the sound hits me like a shock wave. I run out of the dark into the light and out of the silence into the roaring. It's unbelievable. It's like you don't exist one second and you have the whole world the next. Like being born.

We beat Pitt that day, 56-7. I was 8-for-11 passing, and Coach Parseghian told the press afterward: "I had every bit of confidence in Theismann's ability. We know he's small and doesn't measure up to the stature of a Hanratty, but he has plenty of talent."

When Ara said that about my size, I was right beside him, and I raised up on my tiptoes to look down on him. Frightened, nervous, anxious—I had been all of that. But I wasn't paralyzed by it. The challenge excited me. Why should little Joey get killed at Notre Dame? In high school I could outrun most guys, and nobody ever got a clean hit on me. Why should Notre Dame be any different?

After the Pitt game, I started every game throughout my Notre Dame career and broke most of the passing records, including George Gipp's total-offense record. Little Joe wasn't all that little anymore, either, getting up to 177 pounds. My senior year, 1970, Ara said: "Don't ever underestimate Joe. He can pass and he can run; he's a great scrambler and a great leader. He's a winner. And don't let his size fool you. I know other quarterbacks who don't have size, like Lenny Dawson and Johnny Unitas."

Notre Dame gave me so much. It gave me a chance to be part of a great college tradition. And there were so many great players on those teams of 1967–70: Tommy Gatewood, Terry Hanratty, Mike McCoy, Bob Olson, George Kunz, Billy Barz, Denny Allen, Larry Shoemaker, Mike Creaney, Jim Seymour, Bob Kuechenberg, Chuck Zloch, Scott Hemple, Mike Oriard, Joe Haggar, Ed Gulyas, Larry DiNardo, Dan Novakov.

Notre Dame also gave me Joe and Mary Hickey, who kind of adopted me, a kid away from home, as their own. I met them at a barbecue for the freshman football players, and they made their home my home. Anytime I wanted a place to go, they were there. Now we're talking a good Catholic family with a lot of kids. It was great. Joe would be walking around in his boxer shorts and he might have a Scotch and soda in his hand. He'd prop his feet up on the ottoman and wouldn't know who the hell was in his house. He had some of his and some of somebody else's. For me, the Golden Dome was special, and so were Joe and Mary Hickey.

And Notre Dame also gave me Ara Parseghian. Ara saw everything. I was always scared to death of him. He'd have six teams running in practice and he'd be watching from his tower. I'd peek up and he'd be looking the other way, and I'd run a play and suddenly I'd hear his thin, squeaky voice, "Why'd you throw it over there?" It reminded me of my father at 10:30 at night. How the heck did he know?

The first time Ara asked me to come to his office was after my sophomore year. I've met Presidents Ronald Reagan, Gerald Ford, and Jimmy Carter, but only with Ara did I feel as if I were in the presence of royalty. It wasn't so much a young kid's insecurity. Ara was just larger than life. A fiery guy. Cheerleader. Effervescent. Left-handed, so he was always throwing that left fist to the air. He is of Armenian ancestry, so he had a handsome tan glow even in the winter. Dapper. Always in control. The kindly king. The boss.

That day in his office, we chatted only about the season and maybe about classwork. Ara was dedicated to academics for his guys, so much so that Notre Dame even made a student out of me.

In high school I had just goofed around because I had enough smarts to get by. At Notre Dame, though, that all changed. Schoolwork came very hard to a guy who'd rather be shooting pool at the student union. But I made a commitment to study, a commitment that had nothing to do with education. It had to do with staying eligible to play football. I went to Notre Dame strictly to play ball. But after two years, I found out that school wasn't tough if you applied yourself.

Notre Dame is proud of its athletic–academic record. The NFL players' union says that out of 1,500 pro players, about 35 percent actually graduate from college. Notre Dame graduates almost everybody. I got a B.A. in sociology. It didn't make me Einstein, but I am proud of my diploma.

It meant I stayed eligible, and sometimes that meant just

showing up at class. My teacher for freshman math, Jake Kline, the baseball coach, believed that if you came to class every day, you deserved an A. He figured you had to be a stonebrain not to soak up something. Math by osmosis. We called him Straight-A Kline. One guy got a B because he hardly ever came to class.

By my senior year I was a *real* student with grades good enough to be Academic All-America. Still, I was a quarterback, not a rocket scientist. So I took courses such as Speech and Argumentation. For that one we'd sit around talking and arguing. You had to be fast with the words and you had to make a reasoned case. Of all my classes, Speech and Argumentation turned out to be the most beneficial. I got A's and B's. The world can thank Notre Dame for teaching Joe Theismann to speechify and argumentate.

But one of the most important things I learned was taught to me by Roger Valdiserri, the Notre Dame sports information director. He devised rules for interviews, which I remember to this day. These are also rules, alas, that I broke much too often.

Roger's rules: (1) always compliment the opposition; (2) always compliment your teammates; and (3) never take credit for yourself. Roger said, "If you do those things, you pretty much can't get into trouble." These fundamentals seem self-evident. But just in case, Roger would stand across the room, behind the interviewer, and he'd shake his head "yes," answer the question, or "no," avoid that one.

These were great lessons for a kid out of Jersey, and they have helped me for years—except, of course, when they slipped my mind. I sometimes wonder what my life would be like if I always had Roger with me, nodding or shaking his head, telling me when to shut up and when to talk.

I never needed much help or encouragement to speak up, as Coach Parseghian learned early. We beat Pitt and Georgia Tech easily my first two starts that sophomore season of '68, and then came Southern Cal. For me, Southern Cal was the ultimate measuring stick of how good you were. They were like a pro team. They were ranked No. 1 in the nation. They had a running back named O.J. Simpson.

My first pass of that USC game was intercepted by Sandy Durko, who ran it back 21 yards for a touchdown. The game was 40 seconds old and we were behind, 7-0.

As I jogged over to the sidelines, Coach Parseghian just looked at me. I said, "Don't worry about it, I'll get it all back."

In retrospect, I don't know why I said that. I was only a sophomore making my third start in front of Notre Dame's holy ghosts. The game was on national TV, against the nation's No. 1 team. But I said it, and I think it set the tone for the rest of my life. I believed in myself. I believed I could meet any challenge.

I guess I could have said, "I'm sorry," or, "Please don't take me out." But promising to get the TD back were words that just came naturally to me because of the confidence I'd developed with teams that had met all challenges. I'd succeeded at every level from Pop Warner to South River High in baseball, basketball, and football. If you've never lost, you don't worry about losing. You find ways to win. And I was lucky enough for almost 20 years to play with guys whose success and confidence rubbed off on me.

Our center in 1968, Mike Oriard, wrote a book about his football career, *The End of Autumn*. Mike wrote that the skinny new quarterback in '68 could run and throw and was more durable than he seemed. "Joe was also brash, even cocky," Mike said, "but in an engaging manner that exuded confidence rather than conceit."

Sometimes, that confidence got me into trouble, as it would again and again in the years to come. Here I was, this sophomore, yelling and hollering at older players. I just couldn't stand it when mistakes were made. I took it as my responsibility to point out those mistakes.

Lucky for me, my quarterback coach, Tom Pagna, realized the need for a buffer between me and some of the others. When I yelled at a receiver, blocker, or running back, he'd yell at me even louder: "Theismann, would you shut up! You run the team, and let us coach it!" And every once in a while, I did.

So after throwing that interception to Durko, I trotted toward Coach Parseghian and decided to be engagingly confident. By halftime, we were ahead, 21–7. We scored once on a trick play when I handed off to Coley O'Brien at halfback and he threw back to me for a 12-yard touchdown.

A reporter on the sidelines asked what I thought about being ahead. I said, "It's terrific. Do you expect Notre Dame to be anywhere else?"

We ended in a 21–21 tie with the nation's No. 1 team. Ara said, "Theismann, after that incident in the first quarter, must be admired for his courage, the way he came back like that." Reading those words in the newspaper the next day made me feel good, not only about myself but about the team. *We* had come back, not just *I*.

My junior year, we were 8–1–1 and accepted the school's first bowl bid in 40 years. We lost to Texas in the Cotton Bowl, 21–17, and that victory gave Texas the national championship. My senior year we had a real shot at the title; we were undefeated going into our last regular season game—at Southern Cal.

Southern Cal jumped on us hard, 21–7 in the first quarter, and it was 38–14 early in the third quarter. Then it started to rain. It rained like you've never seen it rain. The field was a quagmire. On the sidelines, water came over your shoes. Guys were fumbling the ball all over the place. Ara said to me, "Put it up."

So we did. We threw the wet football all over that swamp. Our last 21 plays were all passes. For the day, I threw 58 passes and completed 33 for 526 yards. Southern Cal's quarterback, Jimmy Jones, couldn't hold onto the ball, and I was throwing it around like it was a sunny Sunday in the park. But we just couldn't score in that rainstorm and lost, 38–28. The ironic thing about that game is that 11 years later, I'd be playing for Southern Cal's offensive-line coach, Joe Gibbs.

The loss killed our chances for the national championship, but we went back to the Cotton Bowl against Texas again, and this time we won, 24-11. We finished with a 10-1 record, and my college career, after starting with negative questions, ended with affirmative answers. In games I started, we were 20-3-2. The All-America voters put me on their first team, and then I held my breath waiting to hear who would win the Heisman Trophy.

Emotionally, my hopes had been built up all season by people saying, "You have a real good chance of winning the Heisman." Everybody around South Bend wore "Theismann for Heismann" buttons. It had affected me so much that I was actually figuring how much the Heisman could mean in dollars when the NFL drafted me.

There were three other logical candidates. Jim Plunkett at Stanford, Rex Kern at Ohio State, and Archie Manning at Mississippi.

The Heisman is 50 percent publicity and 50 percent ability. The voters are newspapermen and broadcasters from all across the country. It figures that they'll most likely vote for the players they know best. So it seemed the Midwest and the South would be split between Rex, Archie, and me. Jim was very strong in the West, and I would lose votes in the Midwest because Rex was close by at Ohio State. No one knew what the East would do. Sounds like political candidates waiting for election returns.

When the telephone rang that afternoon in the Notre Dame sports information office, I figured, "This is it." Instead, the phone call was the start of a seven-year period in which I'd keep wondering if I would ever make it big after college.

The call was to let us know that Jim Plunkett had won. Jim deserved it. He was a great quarterback. But it still was a traumatic moment for me because I wanted that Heisman Trophy so much; I truly thought I had earned it, not only with a good senior year but with a junior season that statistically was the best any offensive player had ever had at Notre Dame. Paul Hornung won the Heisman at Notre Dame when they went 2-8. I lost it going 10-1.

Maybe the change of pronunciation of my name upset some voters who saw that as an opportunistic device. Fact is, all I did was use the true and original pronunciation of the family name brought over from Austria.

After my sophomore year, Roger Valdiserri asked, "How do you pronounce your name?"

A strange question. I said, *"Theesman."*

Roger said, "There's the Heisman Trophy, Joe. And I think we should pronounce your name as *Thighsman."*

I wasn't going to change my name simply because of some trophy. So I called my father. "Dad, how do we pronounce our last name?"

He said, "What?"

"Please, just answer my question, Dad." He said *Theesman.* But he also said my grandmother Eva insists it's *Thighsman.*

I told Roger, "Well, my grandmother pronounces it that way. What the heck, let's do it."

My grandmother, Eva Theismann, said our family name was pronounced *Thighsman* until the Theismanns registered in American schools and the people read the name the easiest way they could—*Theesman.* Grandmother Eva was 88 years old in 1986 when she said, "I am very disappointed in those reporters who say Joey changed his name to win that trophy, whatever it is. It is not true. His name is said *Thighsman.* American kids called us *Theesman* and we didn't care. But now my people are all dying off and I'm glad the name is correct."

Grandmother Eva said she had heard a radio broadcast reporting that I had changed my name to win the Heisman Trophy.

So we called that radio station, and I told them, "Get it straight once and forever. *Thighsman* is how we said it in Austria. *Thighsman* is how we said it on Ellis Island, and *Thighsman* is it."

Grandma also said, "You know, Joey had to go to college to learn how to pronounce his name."

4
How I Traded Three Super Bowls for a Ferris Wheel

Two months after losing the Heisman, I sat in Roger Valdiserri's office again, this time for the NFL draft. The first round went by and the phone didn't ring. This took about an hour. Then another hour passed in the second round. Still the phone didn't ring. Finally, I said: "Goodbye. I'm going to play basketball. Call me when somebody wants me."

By the time the Miami Dolphins drafted me in the fourth round, the message was clear. Everybody thought Joe Theismann wasn't good enough to play with the big boys. Later, some explanations seemed to make sense; not that they pacified me, but I could understand what happened. At a banquet before the draft, I met Pete Retzlaff, general manager of the Philadelphia Eagles. Philly is close to South River. I thought, "Wow, great, the Eagles." After we shook hands, Mr. Retzlaff said, "How tall are you?"

Even today, I don't understand why everyone's so concerned about a quarterback's height. It's a myth. They say a small quarterback can't throw over a 6'5" defensive line-man. The truth is, if your offensive line is creating the passing lanes the way it's supposed to, you never have to throw over anyone. You're throwing *between* the defensive linemen. When people say size is a factor, I ask them to name five great quarterbacks who are 6'3" or more. They can't do it.

Still, here was the general manager of an NFL team asking me how tall I was. I said, "Six feet."

"You look about 5'11". How much do you weigh?"

"One-seventy-five."

"You look about 170," Mr. Retzlaff said. Then he walked away, and that was the last I heard from the Philadelphia Eagles.

A scouting combine called BLESTO-VIII pools infor-mation and opinion for several NFL teams. BLESTO rated me a 1.7: "Expected to make a 40-man roster . . . might improve."

My rating might have been low because I threw poorly in the Hula Bowl all-star game in front of all the scouts. Maybe it didn't make any difference to them, but I had banged up my elbow in the Cotton Bowl and had no feeling in two fingers of my right hand. I couldn't throw a spiral to save my life. Everything went end over end. It was so bad I volunteered to return punts, just so I could play.

In any case, my visions of the Heisman Trophy making me rich as a first-round draft pick in the NFL were gone, like air out of a football. I was left to choose between going to the NFL as a fourth-rounder, or accepting an offer from the Toronto Argonauts of the Canadian Football League.

Before the NFL draft, the Argonauts offered me $50,000 to sign and $50,000 a year for three seasons. Miami's first offer was $17,000 a year. I about died. But then the Dolphins general manager, Joe Thomas, went into the hospital, and the owner, Joe Robbie, got into the negotiations.

Mr. Robbie asked, "What do you want?"

"Thirty-five, 45, and 55, and a $35,000 signing bonus

broken down over three years."

Mr. Robbie said, "Fine."

What? Weren't we supposed to argue? Oh, no. I went cheap. But a deal's a deal. So I stuck it out. And me being me, I went on Miami television to say, "Come hell or high water, I'll be a Miami Dolphin."

What I didn't count on, though, was a rider to the contract drawn up by Mr. Robbie. The rider said I had to repay all of the signing bonus if I ever failed to make the 40-man roster, even in the second or third year of the contract. That wasn't part of any deal I'd agreed to. We argued for weeks, until the Dolphins finally relented, saying, "OK, the bonus is unrelated to your making the team and you don't have to give it back."

But by then I was so disillusioned with the Dolphins and the negotiating process that I had asked the Argonauts if their offer still stood. The money wasn't much more than Miami's offer, but, yes, it still stood and it hadn't changed. Toronto dealt straight with me and I felt Miami didn't.

So I flew to Toronto and, probably to keep me from changing my mind again, Toronto owner, John Bassett, Sr., wouldn't let me leave without signing the contract. He said, "If you leave, the offer is off the table." I signed and asked him not to announce it until I had had a chance to call Don Shula and the Dolphins.

Well, Mr. Bassett owned a newspaper in Toronto as well as some radio stations. He wasn't going to sit on a scoop. It was in the paper and on the air the next morning, as I learned when the phone rang. It was Ara Parseghian saying, "Joe, what have you done? Don Shula is on the line and he is mad as can be. He says you have a moral obligation to the Dolphins. What are you doing?"

"The Dolphins took a hard line, wouldn't budge, and I got tired of it."

The next day, Coach Shula flew to South Bend. Again he said, "Joe, you have a moral obligation to be a Dolphin. You said, 'Come hell or . . .' "

"I'm sorry," I said. "Yes, I agreed to sign with you. But I

didn't sign. I have signed a contract with Toronto."

Gone was the Heisman Trophy. Gone was the first round of the NFL draft. Gone, in fact, was the NFL. One of the great coaches in the history of football was furious with me. And I wound up playing football on a fairgrounds in Canada for a twice-fired coach whose tailor walked the sidelines with him.

You tell me. Is this how Joe Namath got started?

At Notre Dame, you came out of that dark tunnel and you saw 60,000 faces. At Toronto, the first thing you saw was a ferris wheel because the stadium was on the Canadian National Exhibition Fairgrounds. The Canadian Football League was a classy operation, and my three years were fun. But still, there were no Texas Stadiums up there where hockey is king. The ballyard at Regina, Saskatchewan, looked like a converted dogtrack.

Somehow, the Toronto Argonauts were pretty good. Our coach, Leo Cahill, was, and still is, the No. 1 football personality in Canada, a colorful performer who was fired and rehired by the Argonauts so often that his autobiography is entitled, *Good-bye, Leo.*

Leo was a big, heavy guy who liked three-piece suits, like Hank Stram at his fashion-plate best. So he used to invite his tailor, Norm Holland, to the sidelines at games. The tailor was a big, round guy about six feet tall and 285 pounds. They looked like Buddha bookends.

I liked Leo. He had just one problem as a coach. He didn't know squat about football, which he proved my first year by alternating me and Greg Barton, who had come north from the Detroit Lions. By "alternating," I don't mean every other week; it was every other series in a game.

No matter what happened—if we went 99 yards in two plays—Greg would replace me for the next series. And even if he took the team in for a score, I'd replace him. Greg could throw the hell out of a football, but in a game it got a little too exciting for him. Finally, I went to Leo and said: "Leo, this is crazy. We gotta stop this stuff with me and

Greg. One of us has to be the quarterback. And it ought to be me."

Leo said an amazing thing. He said: "If I make you the starter, Joe, I may lose Greg. He may say, 'The hell with it, I'm going back to Detroit.' And if I make Greg the starter, you'll harass the shit out of me. This way I can appease everybody."

Failing at Speech and Argumentation, I went to Plan B. I took Greg to lunch. Every day. All season long we ate hot dogs and drank milk shakes. By year's end Greg had gained 20 pounds and couldn't move around on the field. With my help, Greg ate his way out of the Canadian Football League.

So we've got ferris wheels and dogtracks and Buddha the Tailor, and my competition eats his way out of a job. Wild times on the tundra. What a team. With only 32 guys on the roster—17 Canadians, 15 Americans—we had two Ph.D.s. Paul Desjardins, my center, was a biochemist, my wide receiver, Mike Eben, was an expert in Germanic languages. We also had some American football players, such as Jimmy Stillwagon and Granville Higgins. We even had a running back called "X-Ray" because most of the time he was invisible. He ran so fast no one could catch him.

That first year we played Calgary in the Grey Cup, the CFL's version of the Super Bowl. With four minutes to play, our defensive back Dick Thornton, who'd been a quarterback at Northwestern, intercepted a pass and took it back to the six-yard line. Dicky figured he'd won the car that went to the MVP. Next play, I threw an incompletion. Second play, we ran a sweep with X-Ray—and he fumbled. We lost the ball and the game, and Dick Thornton was mumbling: "If I could get my hands on him, I'd kill him, I really would. I had the car keys in my hand."

The other highlight of 1971 was the birth of my first son Joey on my own birthday. I was content with my situation; conditions were good in the CFL, and it was good enough football that a coach by the name of Bud Grant came out of there and succeeded in the NFL. In the offseason, the CFL asked me to fly to New York to sell American TV rights for the CFL. This was not unlike selling stoves at a shipwreck.

The second year in Canada, I broke my leg in the season opener. Running out of bounds, I pivoted on the artificial turf to take one more peek up the field. Right then somebody jumped on my back, and my foot stuck to the turf. There was a popping sound, and I thought it was the Achilles tendon. I jumped up to jog off the field. But no. Let's sit down. The fibula was broken in two. Because the fibula is the smaller of the two bones in the leg, and because I was 24 years old, the fibula healed in nine weeks. (Yes, the same fibula was broken in 1985. No, it didn't heal so quickly. Yes, old age does make a difference.)

With me sidelined for most of '72, the Argos won only one game and Leo was fired. Our new coach was John Rauch, who had been let go by the Oakland Raiders in '68. John's problem was he didn't understand Canadian football. You only get three downs. John had us run 95 percent of the time on first down. So it was always second-and-10 (which is like third-and-10 in the NFL), and it's hard to get much done when every polar bear south of the Arctic Circle knows you're going to pass.

By then I also was in a contract dispute with the Argonauts general manager, John Barrow, who had been a Canadian All-Star lineman in his playing days. When he offered $75,000 to sign again, I said: "That's not enough. The NFL will pay me that. You have to give me a reason to stay here."

Barrow was angry. "You're just a typical kid who got too much too soon."

To which I replied, "And you're just a washed-up lineman who didn't get anything and is envious about it."

The good news about my third year in Canada was the birth of my daughter Amy in March. The bad news was that all I wanted was out. It had been fun, but I wanted Joe Namath's league. Coming so close in the Grey Cup made me hungry to win a Super Bowl. When I left Canada, I had my own pinkie ring made with my number 7 on it next to three little—*very* little—diamonds—three to remind me of Miami's three Super Bowls and what I had missed.

The only real regret I have about my Canadian journey is that Coach Shula still holds it against me. Working Super Bowl XIX, we went to see the Dolphins practice. Don said, "You know, Joe, you left me high and dry." He wasn't smiling. He wasn't kidding. And I told him I was sorry, because I consider him a great coach, up there with Vince Lombardi and Tom Landry.

In '74 Miami was off my list of prospective NFL teams because Bob Griese was still a young quarterback at the top of his game. The Washington Redskins, on the other hand, had Sonny Jurgensen, who was 40, and Billy Kilmer, 35. I figured I could spend a year or two learning from them and then get my shot.

So I talked to George Allen, the Redskin coach. He took me into his office. I'd never met anyone so enthusiastic. Or so strange. He wrote down everything he was telling me on the back of an envelope. He listed all the reasons I would be the perfect Redskin quarterback. He said: "I want you because you move around. You've got a great arm. You're young. You're durable. You're a winner."

Wow, exciting. Me and George Allen, the great coach. He would trade a No. 1 draft pick to Miami for the rights to me. This was great. I'll do it, George, sign me up. I'll be here. This was it. The big time for little Joey Theismann. Jurgensen and Kilmer were getting old. In a year or two, I'd be the quarterback in the nation's capital.

Yeah. Sure. Little did I know that when Jurgy and Billy went out drinking, it wasn't only from a Jack Daniels bottle. It was from the Fountain of Youth. The next two years were the toughest of my football life.

5
Riding the Pine

My first season in Washington, 1974, the Miami Dolphins came to RFK Stadium to play us in a rematch of Super Bowl VII. If you've never been to Robert F. Kennedy Stadium, you have no idea what a special place it is. A small stadium, with only 55,045 seats, it creates a wonderful intimacy between the fans and players. This day in '74, with the Dolphins in town, there was a soft mist hanging in the air a foot over the stadium turf.

It was a late afternoon game, the sun was going down, and you could smell the popcorn and you could smell the Tufskin and you could smell the grass. It was a real October football afternoon, as perfect as you could order up. To get on the field at RFK you have to walk up through the old baseball dugouts. I knelt on the dugout steps. Looking out there, seeing the mist over the grass, it was like a dream. This was the NFL. At last.

And I didn't play a lick that day. Not with George Allen the coach and Billy Kilmer and Sonny Jurgensen the

quarterbacks. I was the new kid in the retirement home of
the NFL. All those things George wrote on the back of his
envelope, they meant I had to wait. With real football under
way, George didn't trust anybody under 35. In 1974 and
1975, I threw 33 passes for the Redskins. My last season in
Canada, I'd thrown 274 passes as a never-pass-on-first-
down quarterback for John Rauch.

George Allen never wanted me to be his quarterback for
the same reason he never wanted Sonny Jurgensen. We
loved to throw the football; George felt safer running it.
David Israel, then a sportswriter in Washington, once said,
"George Allen plays anal-retentive football." I guess that
meant he liked the running game and wanted to keep the
ball in a safe place. George's ultimate victory would be a
2–0 score. The defense would score and the offense wouldn't
make a mistake.

George forced Sonny to retire after '74. Boy, could Sonny
throw. If you wanted a tight spiral down the field that
would land absolutely perfect, Sonny was your man. A
pure passer. He was the best. I once saw him throw a spiral
30 yards *behind his back*. Try that sometime.

But George wouldn't play Sonny, and he forced him to
quit because Sonny, in George's peculiar mind, was an
uncontrollable spirit. George saw Sonny as the bad boy
who wanted to do things his own way. And since Kilmer
didn't have the throwing ability of Sonny, he would do
whatever George wanted. Sonny was an artist; Billy, a
mechanic.

My problem was, I was more like Sonny, a thrill seeker
who wanted to create situations outside George's system. A
receiver might be open for 15 yards, but I'd run with the
ball just so people would be impressed.

But running loose like that almost ruined me as a pro
quarterback. The coaches doubted my discipline. The
linemen never knew where I was. Our tackle Terry Herme-
ling was always screaming, "Dammit, Theismann, stay in
the pocket. I block 'em in, you run into 'em. I block 'em
out, they run into you. Stand still, for Christ's sake!"

Still, I considered myself as much an entertainer as a football player. Running, making the big play, was exciting. And I was eager to get the fans on my side by being spectacular.

Big mistake. You make the big play one out of 10 times. It was exciting, but counterproductive to winning. It hurt me a lot. The years 1974 to 1977, under George Allen, were wasted years. At home in the closet hung the symbols of those wasted days: two tuxedoes, winter and summer models. I wasn't getting invited anywhere, but I was hoping.

Well, it wasn't a *complete* waste. I did get to meet my boyhood idol, the man whose every move had entranced me, whose every word had been gospel, Joe Willie Namath. Tell you what, folks. I'm lucky Joe never gave up football for the circus, because the way I copied everything he did, I might be a human cannonball by now. It was after an exhibition game at Shea Stadium in '74 that I ran across the field to shake Namath's hand. Little Joey Theismann on the same field with Joe Namath, at Shea Stadium, the same place I used to visit as a boy. Wow.

But that's about all the activity I had on any field. It was obvious George wanted Billy at quarterback with Sonny in the wings, so I decided to spend my time and energy learning football. I ran at wide receiver on the scout team in practice. I was a running back. Half the guys hated me for crossing the picket line (which I'll get to in a moment), so I was an alien, anyway. What the hell, one day I started catching punts just so I'd have something to do. I'd try to catch them behind my back and between my legs and with my eyes shut. All this took place in practice, of course, because George wasn't about to let me screw up in a real game.

So I had to sneak into my first NFL game, against the Giants at RFK in '74. My usual swell job of holding a clipboard was going very well that day when I had a sudden thought. Why not put all that punt-catching practice to good use? We had released one punt returner in

Speedy Duncan, and Kenny Houston, our safety, was too valuable to be catching kicks (in my opinion, if not in George's). I went to special teams coach Paul Lanham and said, "Should I ask George if I can go in to catch this next punt?"

During games, the head coach is lost in his own thoughts. It is a major long-distance phone call to reach him. That's why you see kids hauling miles of headset cords that are attached to the coach. Otherwise, he would get tangled up in the cord, fall down, and strangle himself, or worse, miss the last quarter.

So Paul said to George, "Want Theismann in on the punt?"

George may or may not have said yes before I was dashing onto the field. First thing I heard was a voice yelling, "Where's *he* going?" The Giants noticed me, too. They said things like, "Joe, you lost?" "Hey, warm-ups are over," "You gonna get hurt out here with the big boys, Joey."

Even if George had wanted to, he couldn't have gotten me off that field with an elephant gun. My memory is that I made a phenomenal punt return . . . breaking several tackles, straight-arming linebackers, keeping those flying feet moving . . . for all of two yards. That year I returned 15 punts for 157 yards, and in '75 it was two returns for five yards. Don't feel sorry for me—just pity the poor guy I was blocking for.

Around this time, a *Washington Post* sportswriter named Gerald Strine wrote an article under the headline, "The Golden Boy's a Loser." He meant me. I wasn't even playing a minute a week. And he wrote that. The guy was a horse-racing writer who moonlighted as a football betting "expert." He never spoke to me, he never interviewed anyone, he never came to a practice, and he called me a loser. It reminded me of the Jersey headline saying I'd get killed at Notre Dame. It just made me more determined to win.

Being like Sonny, by the way, was only one of my problems. When I moved to the nation's capital, I made the mistake of bringing my mouth along. Here was a veteran team of rowdy desperadoes who'd been to the Super Bowl just one season earlier. They were called the Over-the-Hill Gang. Now here came this upstart from the Golden Dome, who announced: "I'm not here just to be on the football team. I want to be the starting quarterback."

Not smart.

If Billy and Sonny hadn't been friends before, they became friends fast. They went from being competitors for the quarterback job to not caring who got it as long as it wasn't me. Billy would not say a word to me. If we were on a deserted island and a snake slithered up out of the water, Billy would have confided in the snake first.

In the last regular season game of 1974, we had two wide receivers injured at Los Angeles. Billy came to the sidelines and said to George, "We need three wideouts right now, but everybody's hurt."

I was standing there, a clipboard quarterback who sometimes returned punts, and I said to Billy, "I can play the third wideout."

Kilmer lowered his head for a minute, slowly turned toward me, looked at me as if I were a bug on the windshield, and walked away. I got the feeling he'd rather walk through hell in a gasoline suit than throw a pass to me.

When I finally won the job from Billy in '78, I sat in meetings with him and offensive coordinator Charlie Waller—just the three of us in a room. Charlie would be at the blackboard, Billy would sit behind me. And he never so much as said a word to me. Nothing. If you want to drive someone crazy, sit in the same room with him for six weeks, four hours a day, and not say a word.

Ironic thing is, we're probably more alike than not. We had the same drive, two rams butting heads in a territorial war. I admired Billy. He'd been a great athlete in college. He held basketball scoring records at UCLA. He'd only been a pro one year when he almost lost his leg in an auto accident. His comeback as a Super Bowl quarterback is all you need to know about how tough Billy Kilmer was and what an athlete he had been.

His hands were so small he had to cup the ball in the palm of his hand. He threw a spiral about as often as Halley's Comet passed overhead. To see him run, with that gimpy leg, was to wonder how he did it. His right foot was loose at the ankle. Every step he took the foot wobbled, like it was attached by a thread. But the guy could damn well win football games. Guys would tell me that if Kilmer screamed at you in the huddle, you'd kill somebody else before you'd have him on your ass again.

Kilmer would play hurt. He'd get his nose blown open and get it stitched up on the sidelines so he could go back in there. One week 10,000 people came to RFK with Band-Aids on their noses because Billy had played with a Band-Aid on his schnozz after getting it ripped up. If Billy Kilmer was on the railroad tracks with a train coming, he'd spit on the locomotive. He had that kind of arrogance, and I admired and respected that.

The harder he worked, the redder his face got, maybe from anger, maybe from high blood pressure. The guys called him "Whiskey." But he could fire up a team. Billy knew his job and he would do it, and he left it to other people to do their jobs. That's something I didn't learn for a long, long time.

Bad year, 1974. After alienating Jurgensen and Kilmer, I infuriated most of the other players by crossing their picket line to enter training camp.

The Redskins were the closest, toughest, strongest union team in the NFL. Our center, Len Hauss, a growly, gruff Georgia guy, became the union president. The union went out on strike when training camp opened that year. To them, the strike was a statement of principle. To me, it was an opportunity.

It never occurred to me that by crossing my teammates' picket line, I would make them angry forever. That wouldn't have stopped me, anyway, because I was thinking short-term. I wasn't a union member, I didn't have to strike.

If Jurgensen and Kilmer were on strike, the quarterback job was open.

I said, "I'm going to camp; it's a great opportunity to show my wares." There would be no competition at quarterback. One quarterback in camp was a guy named Clarence Trinkle. Now, I'm sorry, Clarence, but I just couldn't hear the loudspeaker in the stadium announcing "Clarence Trinkle at quarterback for the Redskins." He was a 32-year-old schoolteacher who had played quarterback in his previous life or something. They were just bringing bodies in.

Guys tried to talk me out of going to camp. They said that without me the Redskins would have no quarterback and they'd have to cancel the exhibition game. The union needed that financial leverage. But what did I care about any union? I wasn't a member, I didn't care. All I wanted was the quarterback's job. I told them: "I've waited all my life to play quarterback in the NFL. I'm not going to miss this opportunity because of a picket line."

These were my teammates. There are the guys who would have to put their butts on the line for me. And when I crossed the picket line, they said, "You'll live to regret this." And, "You're a scab, you're hurting us, you better watch your backside."

They never forgave me. I was forever an outsider with the Over-the-Hill Gang. If I ever had the chance to be one of the guys on George Allen's team, crossing the picket line in '74 slammed the door in my face.

The next year, I was still a third-string quarterback who sometimes returned punts and worked as a wide receiver in practice. This was on a team that had Hall of Famers like Sonny Jurgensen and Charley Taylor. We had Larry Brown, the league's MVP in '72. But it was yours truly, the third-string quarterback who opened a restaurant with a modest name: "Joe Theismann's." It was my humble beginnings as "jock of all trades, master of none."

As far as I know, Billy Kilmer never came to dinner at my place.

6
The George Allen Retirement Home for Wayward Warriors

After those first two miserable years with the Redskins, all I wanted was out. I wanted to play. I begged George Allen to trade me. Trade me somewhere, anywhere. Ship me to Tampa Bay or Seattle, the new expansion franchises. That's how desperate I was. I said: "George, please, do me a favor. Trade me to Tampa Bay. I'll play for them for four years, and when I'm older, I'll come back and play for you."

Patience was never one of my strengths, anyway, and here it was 1976, my sixth year out of Notre Dame, and I had thrown a grand total of 33 passes in the NFL. Dan Marino threw more than that before he was old enough to shave. And the worst part was, I saw no hope of ever playing for George Allen, because he was as conservative as I was flamboyant.

When Leo Cahill in Canada wouldn't accommodate me with his quarterbacking job, I developed my take-a-quarterback-to-lunch strategy. Well, in Washington, I knew Billy Kilmer wouldn't even go to McDonald's with me. So it was necessary to come up with a new strategy if I ever wanted to play in the NFL.

It came down to this: I decided to simply and totally defy George Allen. I did everything I could to infuriate him so that (1) he'd trade me just so he wouldn't have to listen to me anymore, or (2) he'd say, "Theismann, get in the game—and I hope you fall on your face."

My dawn-to-dusk talking in those early years was seen by some people as egotistical self-promotion. But my talking, much of it downright stupid, was nothing but a challenge to George Allen to play me and see where the chips fell.

It got me nowhere. All it did was convince the public that Joe Theismann was a spoiled brat, too cocky for his own good, and certainly no asset to any organization that depended, as a football team does, on harmony among its workers. There was some truth in that, too, as you'd have seen if you came out to our practice.

Running the scout team, I did my own thing, not what was best for the Redskins. I tried to beat our defense, which served absolutely no purpose. I went full speed in half-speed drills and threw touchdown passes to wide receivers when the ball was supposed to go short. I tried to turn every day into a Joe Theismann offensive highlight package.

Some of the players were mad, and the coaches were saying, "Joe, you gotta cool it, you gotta stop doing this." But my frustration level was reaching an explosion point. I let off steam in practice, but it wasn't enough. So one night at a banquet, I really did it.

Rusty Tillman, one of our linebackers, invited me to a dinner, where we were supposed to give a little talk and answer questions from the audience. Someone in the crowd asked me about George Allen. My answer began diplomatically. "George Allen is a unique guy, and a winner," I said, and then diplomacy went out the window.

"George Allen is also an egotist. He is unfair. He doesn't give players a chance to prove themselves. I play now because I enjoy the game. I don't play for George Allen."

I thought my remarks that night were limited to the people in that room, but a freelance reporter in the crowd fed the hot-copy quotes to *The Washington Post*. And the next morning, I awoke at 7 A.M. to the headline, "Theismann Doesn't Play for Allen."

Now, in some cities, a quarterback popping off about the coach is no big deal. In Washington, it was a very big deal, because George, with all his winning and all his eccentricities, had become a major news figure. One writer even called him "Nixon with a whistle." And now the second-string quarterback—known generally as cocky, ungrateful, and opportunistic—was attacking Coach Allen.

I had hit rock bottom. I was a loose cannon in practice. I was ostracized by my teammates, and now I had ripped George Allen, the Super Bowl coach, a man who won football games by the dozens.

So at 7:00 that morning, I drove straight to George's house to apologize, scared to death, all the while thinking: "He'll trade me to Green Bay or Buffalo or someplace where the sun never shines. He's gonna exile me to Siberia. And he's got every right to." I thought I was gone for sure.

By the time I got to his home, I was a wreck. No one was home, so I raced to Redskin Park to find him. The first guy I saw was Jake Scott, a buddy of Billy Kilmer's. Jake smiled and said, "Your ass is gone." From the way he said it, it was pretty clear he liked the idea.

When I finally got to George's office, I began: "Coach Allen, I said some things I shouldn't have and I want to take responsibility for it. I said them out of frustration, and I sincerely apologize to you for doing that."

George never got mad. He surprised me by saying: "I appreciate your coming in and telling me. But, Joe, I'm really disappointed. If not playing was bothering you so much, why didn't you take the time to come talk to me?"

I was dumbfounded. Where had this man been? Hadn't he heard me bitching for four years? George acted like this was all new. And although he now knew the full range of my discontent and frustration, he *still* played Billy Kilmer and I *still* held the clipboard.

I was trapped, a prisoner in the George Allen Retirement Home for Wayward Warriors. Are you too old for most NFL teams? Come play for the Redskins. Too beat up? Come to the Redskins. Nobody wants you? George Allen wants you. These guys were the Raiders before the Raiders were the Raiders. This was a pirate ship of old-timers who'd chew a leg off to get out of a bear trap.

These real men were proud of their pain. They considered pain a minor nuisance to be dealt with. You took the needle, which meant getting an injection of the painkiller Xylocaine. Or you'd take the needle to relieve the bloody swelling of a bruise or muscle tear. They'd stick the needle in and blood spouted out like it was an oil well.

Taking the needle. This was a Redskin badge of courage. Coaches would never actually say you *had* to take the needle, they just had a way of making you feel you were letting down your grandmother and your country if you didn't go out there. You can walk, why can't you play? And then you've got the psychological game to deal with. If you don't play, a kid will, and he may keep the job forever.

So gimme the needle, doc. Some guys, you couldn't make them *not* take the shot. You couldn't make them *not* play. They were part of the brigade and they were going over the hill. It didn't matter if they were running into machine-gun fire, they were going.

A big defensive tackle Bill Brundige took the needle and played in six-degree weather with a frostbitten foot. Center Len Hauss played with phlebitis, even though a blood clot could have jarred loose and killed him in the middle of a play. Pat Fischer, the littlest and meanest defensive back you'll ever see, put Tufskin in his mouth. Diron Talbert had the ugliest hands ever attached to a human being, even a tackle. His fingers went in eight different directions. Larry Brown's knees were so bad he could hardly walk, but there have been few better running backs. They all had great hearts. You'd see Ron McDole, 35, chewing on a towel like a nervous kid. Then he'd go out there limping on a bad knee and terrorize people.

Nowadays you get lawsuits over injuries, but in the '70s you accepted the pain as part of the business. If it left you crippled or maimed or in constant pain, tough. To go and play without being hurt, that was nothing. But if you couldn't lift your left arm, you earned the right to hurt the rest of your life and you were proud of it.

If you were to see those old Redskins nude, God forbid, you wouldn't know what you were looking at. An orthopedic disaster area, maybe. But look around a locker room today. Everybody has two or three necks, six or seven biceps, and four legs. These guys are gigantic, and their muscles are defined so they look like statues.

They run the 100 in 9.5. The Over-the-Hill Gang would run the 100 in about a week, and only if you put a keg of beer at the other end. George always said, "OK, everybody get their weight work." People laughed out loud because nobody ever lifted a weight on that team. Those guys used to walk through a weight room and that would be their weight work. They'd feel the iron ions bouncing off their bodies. Mmmmm, good. Time for a beer.

Those guys were the last of the dinosaurs. They're extinct today. There are no more like Hauss and Brundige and Talbert and Kilmer.

My only great moment with these guys came in 1974 when I was on the trainer's table next to Sonny Jurgensen. I had a deep thigh bruise that required drainage. They stuck the needle in and, boy, was I proud. They took the top off the syringe, and the blood just shot out.

Yep, me and Sonny, brothers of the needle. To take the needle, to be shot up with Xylocaine, to have blood drained out, that was it. You were there. You were part of the Washington Redskins. They could hate your guts, but if you took the needle, you could think of yourself as a desperado in the Over-the-Hill Gang.

Ordinary people may think this talk of needles and Xylocaine is bizarre. With George and the Over-the-Hill Gang, the bizarre was commonplace. Until a doctor enlightened him to the dangers of heat stroke, George considered drinking water a distraction on the practice field. George never noticed the guys locked into the fetal position with heat cramps. We used to smuggle out ice and hide it behind the yardage markers. George defied nature. In lightning storms, he'd take his afternoon jog around the practice field. My buddy Pete Wysocki once told him, "I'll run with you, George—if you promise to remember me in your will."

George may be the only NFL coach ever to order a linebacker to shave his legs. Wysocki was in the shower one day after we beat San Francisco. For laughs, Pete had shaved a tuxedo stripe up the side of his legs through a black jungle of hair. Now George comes into the shower. George is superstitious. If we win, everybody sits in the same seat they sat in on the plane. Everybody is in the same chair for meetings. In the shower, Pete saw George staring at him. George was fascinated by the tuxedo stripe. He said, "Pete, you better shave the front, too. We're playing the Giants this week."

George would say that losing is worse than dying because if you die you don't have to think about the next game. He wasn't kidding. He'd die a thousand deaths if we lost. He had a chauffeur, and not because he was a big shot. George couldn't be trusted to drive, because he was always thinking about how to stop the Packers or Roger Staubach. If the man had to drive his own car, he wouldn't have lived five days. He'd be in a ditch or up a tree.

Every minute of George Allen's day was devoted to winning. On his desk he had a little sign that asked, "What have you done today to make the Redskins a winning team?"

George had that voice that always sounded hoarse. He talked almost in a whisper, like he was giving away national CIA secrets. He squinted his eyes into slits. The effect was comical, although he certainly meant to be dead earnest. At a team meeting before a Dallas game, George rasped, "Oooh, I just wish it was me and Tom Landry at the 50-yard line." He balled up his hands into fists and shook them in the air.

Dallas always got George fired up. He'd call on guys in team meetings, demanding to know how they felt about the Cowboys. George would call on Len Hauss, who would say, "I know if we put our hats on 'em, they'll wrinkle."

Now George came to Calvin Hill, who once played for the Cowboys. Calvin is one of this world's fine people, a theology major from Yale with a graying beard that made him look like an Old Testament prophet. George said, "Calvin, what do you think of Dallas?"

There came from the prophet's mouth 10 minutes of words with several syllables each. Calvin wound up his sermon by saying, "And I believe the Dallas organization is an example of man's inhumanity to man."

George never called on Calvin again.

Coach Allen was also a karate fanatic. One day he brought in some boards. They had a big "C" on them. Being an intelligent football player from an outstanding academic institution, and knowing we would play Cincinnati that week, I assumed the "C" stood for Cincinnati.

George has someone hold up one board and says, "You gotta want to beat the Bengals, you gotta want it. This board is the Cincinnati Bengals." He karate-chops it. Yaaaaaaa! And he breaks the board.

Next he takes two boards and says, "You gotta want it real bad. This board represents Paul Brown. I hate Paul Brown." Yaaaaaa! George chopped two boards in half.

Now he has somebody hold up three boards. "It isn't bad enough to just go out and beat someone. You gotta want to annihilate them. You gotta bury 'em, you gotta bust 'em up." Yaaaaa!

Only this time the boards don't break. Blood is trickling down his hand. Poor George, he stood there completely mute, not saying a word, just staring at the board. Finally, he dismissed us. When he came to practice later, nobody said a word. The only telltale sign was a Band-Aid on his hand.

George believed that everyone should share his obsession with winning. Wysocki's mother had a heart attack and Pete needed to be with her early one week, but George didn't want him to leave town. There was yet another of George's game-to-end-all-games coming up Sunday. George asked, "Why do you have to miss practice?"

Pete said: "Sorry about that heart attack, George, but they're going around. Mom happened to pick it up. Yes, I know. My mom's dying, but I really should be thinking about the Giants because this week's game is the most important thing in the universe."

Then Pete left to be with his mother.

The strange thing is, if George Allen had a young team, I don't think his bizarre obsessive behavior would have worked. Players would have said: "This is ridiculous. Get this guy a straitjacket and get us a coach." It's not that the old guys did or didn't take George seriously. They just didn't pay much attention. They let George go on and say the things he had to say. Right after the Watergate stuff, Rusty Tillman wore a Richard Nixon mask to a team meeting, and George didn't even notice.

Our old guys played hard, and I'm sure one reason was that George paid them well. If you pay a guy $50,000 more than he's worth anywhere else, the coach can stand up there in a clown suit and nobody would care.

One thing about George Allen, though. He was a successful coach, and is considered by many to be an offensive genius. He had his own way of doing things and they worked. Question: then why isn't he coaching today? I have a theory about that. When Commissioner Rozelle changed the rule affecting player trades, it forever changed George's methods. Under the rule, you could sign any free agent after his contract expired, without having to compensate his former team. Under the new rule, however, before you could even talk to a free agent, you'd have to give up a draft choice based on his salary. The more he made, the higher the draft choice—which meant if you didn't have high draft choices to trade away, you couldn't get veteran ballplayers.

So George had lived by the trade and now it seemed he would die by it. He had traded away most of the Redskins' top draft choices in order to assemble the Over-the-Hill Gang, and as a result, it seemed that no team would hire him for fear of losing all of *their* draft choices. It wasn't that George Allen could no longer coach, but that his philosophy—"Give me older players who don't make mistakes and I can beat anybody"—became outdated.

Playing for George Allen was absolute heaven. Light practices. No weights. Ice cream and cake every Thursday if you win. TVs and tape recorders to the MVPs of a game. If you were over the hill, if you were not wanted anywhere else, if you were a rebel or misfit, you could be a Washington Redskin for George Allen. You could die and go to Redskin heaven.

On the other hand, it was hell for a certain quarterback who in 1977 was 28 years old and still on the outside looking in.

7
Quarterback at Last

I t was during a Monday night game in 1977—the first
year George Allen really allowed me to compete for the
quarterback job—that I had the wind knocked out of
me. George sent in Billy Kilmer. I quickly said, "I'm ready
to go back in." George said, "Let Billy finish the series."

The next time we got the ball, Kilmer and I both ran
onto the field. We got to the huddle at the same time and
looked at each other like, "What are you doing here?" And
Billy jerked his thumb at me, as if to say, "Get outta here."

This was Monday Night Football, Howard Cosell speaking, and Billy Kilmer had ordered me off his field. It was no
place for a fight, and I didn't have many friends in the
huddle who would be sticking up for me. I ran off the field,
humiliated.

Ray Schoenke, a veteran guard, came over to me during
practice the next week and said: "Don't get mad about what
happened. You'll have your day."

That was nice of him, but Ray was preaching patience to
the wrong guy. I didn't want to wait for Kilmer to go on

Medicare; I wanted to play now. The maddening thing was, I felt I had won the job. I was the No. 1 quarterback. I had beaten out Billy in fair competition in camp. This was not some delusion on my part. I had it from a good source—George Allen himself.

Early in that '77 season, Coach Allen told me, "You're my No. 1 quarterback." Wow. Bells and whistles. Strike up the music. Next stop, the Super Bowl. Then George said something odd, even by his standards. "But don't tell anybody, they'll get upset."

What? Why did he bother telling me? He took the happiest moment of my life and turned it into a deep dark secret. George wanted his decision kept secret, I believe, so he could change back to Kilmer if he didn't like the way it was going with me. He didn't want to announce that he gave me the job permanently because he had sensed the team's sentiments about me. This way the blame would all fall on me, if I wasn't good enough to do the job. OK. He could say anything he wanted, as long as I got to play.

We won five of the eight games I started; we were 7–5 and still in the playoff picture with two games to go. Then George told me: "I'm going to start Billy against St. Louis this week. He has a great history against them and so we're going to play him." History? How are you supposed to develop a history when you don't get to play?

Kilmer, 38 years old, started those last two games, and we won them both but still missed the playoffs.

Then George, in effect, was fired. He was in a front-office squabble with Edward Bennett Williams, who at that time ran the Redskins for Jack Kent Cooke. EBW withdrew a contract offer George had agreed to the previous summer. So George went right to the Rams, only to be fired before the first game. The Rams' owner, Carroll Rosenbloom, said he was worried about George's mental well-being.

George and his wife, Etty, had been nice to me personally. I just wasn't George's kind of quarterback. My buddy Pete Wysocki said: "You don't put escargot on a peanut-butter-and-jelly sandwich. George likes the plain, keep-it-simple, no-mistakes thing. Joe is gourmet ingredients.''

If George Allen had continued to coach the Redskins for another 10 years . . . oh, Lord, I can't even think about it. Let's just say I would have been the best clipboard holder in the league.

My professional quarterback education began the day Joe Walton came to town in 1978 as the offensive coordinator for our new head coach, Jack Pardee. Jack had been a linebacker for George Allen. He was a defensive specialist who left the offense to Joe Walton.

I called Joe Walton "Pops" because he reminded me of my dad. Even today, I feel I'm part of Joe's family. I love that guy. Now he's the head coach of the New York Jets, and I wish him the best of everything. He's sincere, honest, and he cares about the guys who play for him.

Feisty and combative, tobacco-chewin' Pops had been a small tight end for the New York Giants in the '50s and '60s. He always wore his ball cap turned around backward, a symbol of his concentration. And he always seemed to be concentrating on me.

In New Orleans once, I came up short running for first down on third-and-three. As I got to the sideline, Pops screamed, "Why didn't you get the first down?"

"Because I've got a pulled groin. I can't run."

"I don't give a damn. CRAWL if you have to! Just get that first down!"

He saved my career. His offensive system was not only exciting, it was efficient. He knew how to use the Redskins' material. First of all, we had John Riggins, whom George Allen had totally misused as a blocking back. Here was one of the greatest runners ever, and George used him to block for a halfback named Mike Thomas.

Joe Walton wanted to give the ball to John, and he wanted me to be a mobile quarterback who could throw short accurately. Under Joe's discipline, I became a 60-percent passer. God-given talent had pulled me through most athletic situations. But no one in the pros had ever taught me how to play quarterback. No matter how independent you think you are, you still need guidance if you're going to play quarterback in the NFL. Under George Allen, I called my own plays, but in doing my own thing, I never reached my full potential. My growth as a quarterback began only when I gave myself up to Pops and did exactly what he told me to do.

Every Monday Pops and I would have a private quarterback seminar. He'd have a yellow pad on his desk, five pages of mistakes I'd made in the Sunday game—and this could be from a game in which I played well. Five pages of mistakes! Every play was broken down, what went wrong, what went right.

Even if I threw three touchdown passes, one might have been off the sixth step of a drop instead of the seventh. Sometimes I'd go see Pops feeling great, only to walk out feeling like garbage. Other times, if I'd played badly and knew it, he'd find a way to pat me on the back. He knows how to handle people. He'd say, "I'm going to say things to you here that I'm not going to say in front of the team." But one on one, he'd tear me to pieces.

He took this time to make me a better football player. Much of the success I achieved in football, I owe to Joe Walton. He taught me how to think in a game, how to analyze my technique, how to move. A quarterback's three-step drop correlates to a five-step pattern by the wide receiver. A five-step drop correlates to a 10- or 12-yard pattern. A seven-step drop is a 15- or 18-yard pattern.

That's simple math. By the time you drop back so many steps, the receiver also has taken a certain number of steps. If you throw the ball properly, it arrives as the receiver finishes his assigned route.

Before Pops got to me, I might take a 3½-step drop or a 6-step drop or who knows how many steps? Who counts steps? I never did. But Joe Walton counted them and he taught me to count them. Like magic, I got into synch with my receivers. Amazing. Genius is simple stuff that nobody ever notices.

We had a special relationship even after he left. The night

I was waived by the Redskins in 1986, I tried to call him at the Jets' training camp. I was crying. I told his wife, Ginger, "Please tell Pops I want to thank him for everything he has done for me."

Some people want to be doctors or lawyers or presidents. I wanted to be a quarterback. All my life I looked for the secret to making that dream come true. In high school, I wore black high-top shoes because Johnny Unitas and Y.A. Tittle wore black high-top shoes. When Joe Namath showed up in white shoes, so did I. I walked like Namath, all hunched over, taped my shoulder pads in front the way he did, wore a cage face mask like his. I even wanted his bad knees because everyone talked about Joe's knee operations and how he'd fought through pain and adversity to be a great quarterback.

Damn, I was so healthy. Why couldn't my knees have zipper scars from hours of surgery? I was stuck being a healthy, strong, white Anglo-Saxon Protestant quarterback.

I went as far as to believe that the secret to being a good quarterback was a cut-off T-shirt like Kenny Stabler's. Yeah. That's what made Stabler so great in the last two minutes, his black T-shirt. Whatever it took to be a quarterback, I thought for sure it wasn't enough just to be me.

Kids think this way because their lives haven't taken shape yet. They're looking for a model, for a style. Trouble was, I was still thinking this way when I was 29 years old.

Then a bright idea came to me. Maybe there was more to football than how you looked. A radical idea, but you're talking to a Notre Dame grad who got straight A's from Jake Kline. Maybe it was time to talk to somebody who really knew how to throw a football.

One day I asked Sonny Jurgensen: "How do you hold a football? Is there a certain way you grip it?"

Sonny said, "You pick it up."

Hmmm. *You pick it up.* Terrific. This is great information. This is invaluable. I have seen the light. *You pick it up.*

Sonny said, "Just pick it up and throw, whatever feels

natural."

The simple advice is the best. Sonny was right. Now when I do clinics and kids ask me how to hold the ball, I say, "Just pick it up, grip the ball, and throw it any way that feels comfortable."

Face masks, high-top shoes, and cut-off T-shirts—not the answer. Namath, Unitas, Stabler, Starr, Jurgensen—all had something you couldn't buy at the sporting goods store. They had the respect of everybody. I had nobody's respect. Worse, I didn't have even my own respect.

Then, thank God, Joe Walton finally made me into the only quarterback I could be. Me.

I wasted four years under George Allen trying to be somebody else, anybody else. Joe Walton's patience and discipline were the keys. He liked me. He didn't think I was hopeless. I could be myself with him. I could be the real Joe Theismann—but I had to work real hard at being the best Joe Theismann possible.

In my mind, the great Redskin successes began with Joe Walton. He made me into a pro quarterback, and he gave the ball to John Riggins. Pops put into place the two pieces of the offense that later helped us to be winners.

Only later did the Redskins become Super Bowl champions. Only later did I become the Most Valuable Player in the NFL in a year when we made it to the Super Bowl a second straight time. Only later did we set league records for scoring.

Joe Gibbs and his staff would get credit for all that, and they deserved it. Credit also belonged to our general manager, Bobby Beathard, and he deserved it. Victory has a thousand fathers, and I feel Joe Walton deserves credit, too.

We went 8–8 in Jack Pardee's first season, 1978. That was Beathard's first year, too. Bobby was making trades, signing free agents, doing anything to rebuild the team.

In '79 I was lucky on one of two counts: my son Patrick was born, but we weren't good enough to get into the playoffs. Riggins gained over 1,000 yards, I passed for almost 2,800, and he and I accounted for 33 touchdowns between us.

But we didn't make the playoffs because we lost the last game of the season to the Cowboys, 35–34. They got two touchdowns in the last two minutes. Riggins was incredible that night, too. He ran 22 times for 151 yards. He broke one 66 yards for the touchdown that put us up, 34–21. What a run that was. He took an inside handoff and broke it around the entire Dallas defense and outran everybody.

Still we lost, and that game, I believe, broke Riggins psychologically. He sat out the next season, refusing to report unless the Redskins guaranteed a year of his contract. John must have thought, "I can't do any more than this." He gave so much and we came up totally empty.

Riggins was unique, and not just because he was a 6'2", 240-pound running back. That night against the Cowboys, he played at a level above everybody else. He had the amazing ability to do that in tough games.

Some of us need to play at our very best *all* the time because we can't win with anything less. But some guys instinctively know how much they have to give. John had that. He was that good, that great an athlete. And just when you thought he couldn't possibly do any better, he would rev it up another notch. John was incredible when it came down to those nitty-gritty games you had to win. John was superhuman when he needed to be. He knew exactly how much he had to pull from himself, and for that Dallas game in '79 he pulled it all up. He played one of the greatest games ever.

When he sat out the next season, I felt betrayed. The offense was created for John and me. It was a 50–50 proposition, and suddenly half the partnership walked out. John and I were never close personally, maybe because we were in competition for headlines and there was an inevitable jealousy between us. But I admire John tremendously, as much as any ahtlete I've ever played with, and even as angry as I was about his walkout.

I never tried to talk him out of it. It was his business, not mine. He said it was a contractual problem. He wanted guaranteed money and they wouldn't give it to him.

Should I talk to him about it, I asked myself. Would it change his mind? Probably not. It all came down to egos, anyway. There was no way I was going to beg John Riggins to play. No way I was going to tell him my future depended on him.

"John's gotta do what John's gotta do, and I respect that," was my quote to the press. But I didn't feel that way at all, and saying the truth at that time would only have stirred up feelings that would hurt the team even more. You talk about going into the season with a negative attitude. We all did. We went from a 10-6 team to a 6-10 team. And Jack Pardee and his staff, including Joe Walton, were fired.

The last week of that season, we were on the road in St. Louis just trying to get it over with. We'd lost four in a row one time and five in a row another time to go 3-10. By then it seemed pretty clear from reading the papers that Pardee would be fired no matter what happened the last three weeks. Somehow we won two straight before going into St. Louis—and who shows up in the hotel bar? John Riggins. Unshaven. In farm clothes. Looking grungy. Having a drink with a couple of buddies from the team.

Tell you what, Riggins showing up in St. Louis took some gall. He walked out and now he was walking back in 15 weeks later when the ship was about to sink. I saw him in the bar, but we didn't talk. Hell, the damage was done. He missed being around the guys, the camaraderie. Maybe coming by was his way of saying he made a mistake.

It isn't fair to say John Riggins got Pardee and his staff fired. There were still 45 of us and a coaching staff working to win every week, and we failed. But it is fair to say we were 10-6 with John in '79 and 6-10 without him in '80. And it was evident there would be some changes. Every time a new coach is hired, there's always the chance that he'll want to bring in his own man at quarterback. Those three years had been an investment, and I hoped the Redskins weren't going to write them off as bad ones.

By 1980, I'd been the Redskins' starting quarterback three seasons, improving my statistics each year. And I remember the moment I knew the job was mine for good. It was '78, and I had had my bell rung pretty good. The coaches thought I needed to come to the sideline for a minute, and they sent the second-string quarterback trotting onto the field. It was Billy Kilmer. Even if I'd been seeing triple, I wouldn't have come out of that game. I waved Billy back to the bench. I was, at last, the Redskins' quarterback.

8
Jock of All Trades, Master of None

As a kid, I wanted to be a football star. Later, I wanted to be a multimillionaire, a Hall of Fame quarterback, and a happy father and husband. There was even a time in my giddiness when I thought, hey, if Hollywood came along . . . well. . . .

So in 1978, I went to Los Angeles for a screen test. Billy Kilmer sniffed, "What's he going to be, Mickey Mouse?"

No, I was going to be George Raft's bodyguard in *The Man with Bogart's Face*. Mr. Raft played an aging gangster, and I was his bodyguard, a tough dude showing off my alleged macho muscles in a T-shirt three sizes too small. The man who had Bogart's face slapped me upside the head, punched me in the stomach, and left me sagging in a corner. Not exactly Clark Gable, but a guy's gotta start somewhere and *The Man with Bogart's Face* was my first movie in a two-movie career.

My first day on that film, I got to the set at noon, only five hours before my call. I sat talking to George Raft for hours, about everything from how to be an actor to how to pick the ponies.

One night we had to shoot a fight scene on a boat. I wanted to do my own fight scenes and my own stunts. Very macho. When I got beat up by the Bogart-looking guy, I cut my back sliding down against a locker. I thought, "My God, this is worse than football." But that night, I really wanted to get thrown off the boat.

"Yes, I want to do this stunt," I told the director.

Someone pointed out that there were big rocks in the water.

I said, "Naah, let the stunt man do this one."

From there, it was a short move up to being a trucker who saved the lives of seven beautiful girls in a TV show, "BJ and the Bear." I even had two lines. We're talking the rumble and roar of serious ego massage.

My mouth had always preceded my performance. I wasn't a real NFL quarterback until 1978, but you'd never have known it by listening to me. I was selling Joe Theismann long before I sold myself as a starting quarterback. I sold Joe Theismann 100 percent of the time. Washington was a town dedicated to self-promotion, and I joined the crowd.

I did anything: reporter, disc jockey, and commercial pitchman for anything animal, vegetable, or mineral. I made speeches to foot doctors and bankers, to computer salesmen and travel agents. I wrote a book called *Quarterbacking*. In 1975 I opened the restaurant. I was everywhere, talking all the time. If you cracked a window to get fresh air at night, you heard me talking.

You could call me presumptuous or pushy or brash. To me, it was a matter of survival, preparation for the day when I couldn't play anymore. Because the average NFL career lasts less than four years, you better be thinking ahead.

So instead of going out with the guys for a beer, I'd do a commercial or make an appearance or talk to someone about a business deal. This rubbed a lot of people the wrong way. George Allen even asked me not to do commercials because it was upsetting the team. The truth was, yes, it was an ego trip, and maybe it was overdone, but I enjoyed the work and the challenge of business. And I felt that if other guys didn't want to take advantage of the opportunities that were available, then fine. I would.

You have to understand how important the Redskins are in Washington to understand how a third-string quarterback fresh out of Canada can wind up with a restaurant bearing his name. Washington has no baseball team after losing the Senators not once but twice. Pro basketball and hockey are played at the Capitol Center, located outside of the city. Georgetown has a great basketball team, but how many people can fit into a college gym? Meanwhile, the Redskins have sold out every game at RFK Stadium since 1966.

The Redskins are as much a part of Washington as the White House and the Lincoln Memorial. If you look up in Jack Kent Cooke's box at any game, you're liable to see senators and congressmen and Supreme Court justices as well as presidents.

The Monday night after the Camp David accords in 1978, Jimmy Carter came to our game against the Cowboys. We won, 9-5, and *The Washington Post*'s top story on page one the next day began, "Was Camp David this much fun?"

In later years, at the height of my career, I met Jimmy Carter. You can tell when you meet someone whether he is talking to you or whether he doesn't know you exist. Mr. Carter seemed to look right through me, and I knew then what other people meant when they said he was distant and cool.

I also met Gerald Ford, at a charity dinner in New Orleans; I was impressed by his warmth and candor. Ronald Reagan was the most terrific of all. I was fortunate enough to be invited to dinner at the Reagan White House; we talked football, and I had the honor of sitting next to Mrs. Reagan. Father Hessburg presented the President with an original copy of the movie *Knute Rockne: All-American*.

Presidents come and go, along with bureaucrats, journalists, and military people. But the Redskins are a permanent institution everyone can rally around. Once, when we beat the St. Louis Cardinals, George Allen said, "This is a great victory for us, for the city of Washington, and for the nation."

For a Redskin, then, that mania made Washington a good place to take a shot at an outside business. So naturally I was interested in '75 when I heard that some investors wanted to open a restaurant with a Redskin player's name on it.

"Why," one investor said to me, "should we use your name? You're a third-string quarterback and punt returner who talks too much."

I said: "I don't plan on staying a third-string quarterback. And when I'm not third-string anymore, I won't be the punt returner, either. And as for 'talking too much,' it might be good for business."

They gave me 13 percent of the deal for the use of my name. It all sounded glamorous, the kid quarterback with his name in gold script on a restaurant. Fact is, it really was a gamble, because I quickly learned a basic truth about business. Thirteen percent of nothing is nothing.

Six months into the operation, we had made no money, and when I asked the company president to show me the books, he produced a half-sheet paper with some numbers scratched on it. The more questions I asked, the more he squirmed, until finally he resigned and took all the money left in the company. He said it was repayment of a loan he had made.

So, "Joe Theismann's Restaurant" had no money in the bank, and we owed about $30,000 in back taxes. Some glamorous deal, huh? It occurred to me to just walk away from it, just sell out. But I couldn't admit to having failed in my first business venture. I decided to stick with it, and we worked harder than ever.

My partners, Vernon Grandegeorge, Tom Craft, Jim Robertson, and I put the restaurant on its feet and even made a profit the first year. The profit was only $3,000, but it's better than being $30,000 in the hole. By 1987 that $3,000 had turned into a multimillion-dollar operation with three restaurants.

I'm proud of what we've accomplished, and yet my business deals somehow created an image of a guy who only used football to make money outside the game. If you want to say Joe Theismann is a self-promoter, that's fine. The restaurants do have my name on them and publicity is important. But I don't believe that my business work ever detracted from my football. I'm no rocket scientist, but I was smart enough to know I had to stay good at football because football made it all possible.

Yes, it's true: once upon a time, for a fee, I'd endorse anything. One real winner was for a carpet company. I wore this dandy white sport coat with three-inch black checks on it. I looked like a test pattern. Another loser was a singing commercial with the Bullets' star, Elvin Hayes, for *The Washington Star*. Six months later, the paper folded. Our singing put a whole company out of business.

There were other commercials I'm very proud of. My favorite was a United Way spot with my daughter Amy. I also had fun doing a commercial for Russell Athletics, which manufactures and sells sportswear. In the commercial, Ed "Too Tall" Jones picks me up and hangs me in a locker. For the big guy, they wanted a strong, silent type, opposite me, the small, not-so-silent type. In the spot, I'm jabbering away about how good Russell clothes look just hanging in the locker. Ed comes by, and, just to shut me up, he hangs *me* up in the locker.

(Psst, don't tell anybody, but Ed wasn't strong enough to pick me up. They used a lift under me.)

For maybe three years I beat my brains out strutting around before deciding the humiliation wasn't worth it. Of all the ego trips I've been accused of, the "acting" experience was the real thing. I had no real desire to act, no preparation, no foundation, no sense of acting. Cathy Lee would later tell me, "Acting is an art, and you have to love it to put in all the work it takes to succeed." Art? The only art I knew was Art Monk.

My last fling with showbiz came when Burt Reynolds asked me to be in his movie *Cannonball II*. He also invited along Frank Sinatra, Sammy Davis, Shirley MacLaine, Dom DeLuise, Susan Anton, Mary Lou Henner, Catherine Bach, Jamie Farr, and a dozen others. Some critics called it the worst movie ever made. But I'm sure they weren't talking about the blond tow-truck driver who looked vaguely like Joe Theismann. After all, I had six lines of dialogue.

At training camp in Carlisle, Pennsylvania, the local movie house put this sign up on the marquee: "Cannonball II starring Joe Theismann." Embarrassing? Totally.

What I eventually learned was that I didn't like movie work at all. I'd never done anything so boring. You really have to be dedicated to it, like any other job, because all you do is stand around and wait for your scene. You wait all day to work one minute. And that's the *good* part.

The bad part is selling yourself. My agent and friend, Budd Moss, tried his darndest to get me work. Budd took me by the hand and walked me through the hallways of 20th-Century Fox, Universal, Paramount, MGM. We stuck our heads into production offices and said, "Do you need Joe Theismann for your next movie?"

We're selling Joe Theismann like a used car or cheap carpet—and nobody's buying. I'd read for a part, and they'd say, "No, your hair's the wrong color." "No, you're too muscular." "No, you're not muscular enough." "Your eyes aren't right." "We want an older person." "We want a younger person."

Did I need this? Did I need anybody telling me my hair was the wrong color? No. No more movies for this kid. I had accomplished a lot in football, and that's where my life was. So in the end, I made a deal with the entertainment world. Dustin Hoffman plays Willy Loman, I play football.

9
Armed and
Dangerous

Any talk about quarterbacks ought to start with the snap from center. So here's the truth about the snap: I like a hard snap from a center with a big wide rear end. Russ Grimm is my idea of a great center. Besides being a great blocker, he is 6'3" and 290 pounds. I didn't realize how big Russ was until our regular center, Jeff Bostic, got hurt and Russ moved over to center from guard. He's a half-man bigger than Jeff. His posterior is a whole cheek wider. I'm telling you, it was like standing behind a house and having somebody hand you the football through the back door.

For a quarterback, it's a comforting thing to see a big wide butt protecting you from the bad guys across the line. Perhaps I should qualify one thing here. I had Johnny Carson snap me a ball once on the "Tonight" show, and I told him: "Just because I spend half my life with my hands in someone else's rear end doesn't mean we're emotionally involved."

No, sir. In the NFL, there are no "wussies" playing

quarterback. Quarterbacks are cocky guys who take charge, the way Billy Kilmer did. Ol' Whiskey had a leg nearly torn off in a car wreck, but he never lost his quarterbacky arrogance, and he not only came back—he took the Redskins to their first Super Bowl.

When the game is on the line, you want a quarterback who can pull his team out of the fire. And only the quarterback can do that because only he gets to handle the ball on every play.

It's an art form to be taken as seriously as any musician, painter, or writer takes his work. From the stands, you see a quarterback and you see the way he throws the ball down the field, but there's more to it than that. There's ballhandling, faking, reading the defense, and knowing where your receivers are going to be. There's the thrill of being at the controls.

Racing driver Jackie Stewart said that when he drove well, everything went by slowly—even at 180 miles per hour. But if something went wrong, all hell broke loose. The same thing happens at quarterback. When a team is going good, it's effortless. But if something breaks down, it gets to be a lot of hard work.

Then it's up to the quarterback to get the team back on track. Not to demean any other position, but the quarterback is critical. It's a dependent job, dependent on everyone else performing. If the quarterback doesn't do his job, even a perfect game by the other ten guys isn't going to win for you.

It boils down to the quarterback's self-confidence. He'd better want the load on his shoulders. He'd better think he's the best, or he's going to be overwhelmed by the job. What he'd better be is somebody like Sonny Jurgensen, who went to Johnny Unitas's new restaurant, "The Golden Arm," and told Unitas, "Thanks for naming your place after me." What a quarterback had better be is somebody like Hose Manning.

Hose Manning is a fictional quarterback dreamed up by the author Dan Jenkins in his book *Semi-Tough*. Jenkins called Hose "the best milker on the farm," meaning he was the best quarterback in pro ball.

"Hose is a tough leader," Jenkins wrote. "And Hose is not bad-looking for a guy with an Oklahoma face. He's got deep creases in his face and what's left over from a childhood case of semi-acne. He's got black, stringy hair, and he's about the only quarterback left who wears high-top shoes. He's over six feet and weighs about 200. He's got a quick release and he throws what we call a light ball. The nose is up and it's easy to catch. The only thing Hose lost in that car wreck lately was one kidney."

Tough leader, Hose was. Threw nice. Had a bad body.

Billy Clyde Puckett, the hero of Jenkins's book, said his team's quarterback, Boyce Cayce, had cut down a lot on fights in bars. Also, he hadn't stolen a city bus in a long while, and, Puckett said, "You don't hear so much about Boyce's drinking in public or his betting."

Now we're getting somewhere. Fistfights and Jack Daniel's and giving the points. To read this stuff, you'd think quarterbacks have no regard for their own welfare. My own inventory of pain and suffering isn't much alongside some guys' hospital charts, but it may give you an idea of what a quarterback can expect in the NFL: I've been knocked out four times and had my nose broken seven times. I have a staple in my left shoulder holding it together. I have broken my right leg twice. I have broken three ribs on my left side and two on the right. I have torn cartilage in a knee, thanks to the Atlanta Falcons, and the Dallas Cowboys separated my left collarbone. Among the everyday items are bruised metatarsals and sprained toes.

Yet every Sunday, if you're a quarterback, you'll be back out there. You'll let those big bullies take their best shots at you. And you'll keep right on trying to find a way to fling the hoghide to somebody open in the end zone when it means the most.

Jim McMahon, in 1985, did that about as well as any milker ever. He did the John Riggins thing, by raising the level of his performance to whatever was necessary to win games. The great ones do that, and then it's OK for them to say, as McMahon has said: "I'm cocky, yes, and a little bit of a hot dog. But again, I don't think these are necessarily bad traits. The guys who see me day in and day out, my teammates, know my cockiness in a different way. They know I can't stand to lose, that I can't stand to lose because I'm not accustomed to it, and that I don't plan to lose. . . . I'm a winner. There."

Jim may say those things more directly than some would, but if you put every good quarterback under oath you'd get the same testimony. Ask Joe Montana and Dan Fouts. Ask Terry Bradshaw and Bob Griese, Roger Staubach and Kenny Stabler. They're the best of my era in the NFL. They'd all tell you they could get you a touchdown in the last minute to win a Super Bowl.

McMahon's greatest asset is his ability to make the big play. It's easy to say that almost any quarterback could have won the 1985 world championship with that Bear team, and I did make the remark. But Jim's injury in '86 showed how much he meant to that team. Without him, they lost their first playoff game.

Jim's only problem is that his body won't let him play enough to establish himself as a great quarterback. He has always had injury problems, even before Charles Martin of Green Bay body-slammed him in '86 and reinjured Jim's shoulder so badly that he needed surgery. In my opinion, Martin should have been suspended for the whole season. There's no way that should be allowed, and it's up to Commissioner Rozelle to get the message across with heavy fines and suspensions that cost players big money. Jim McMahon's career might have been ended—and Martin was back playing in two weeks. Somehow that just doesn't seem right.

I can laugh about my relationship with Jim now, but we had our own encounter after the '85 season.

Besides winning the game easily, Jim had entertained the media all week. One day he dropped his pants and mooned a helicopter passing over the Bears' practice. He wore punker shades to press conferences and slouched around, talking dirty, a Jack Nicholson-does-the-Super Bowl routine.

That winter, when someone asked what I thought of Jim, I said: "If it weren't for football, he'd be some yo-yo out there drinking beer. . . . There is a responsibility to the youth. Doesn't he realize that kids look up to him? Maybe he doesn't care."

These comments were directed at him as a result of the now-famous headband incident, which occurred after the Commissioner had asked him not to wear his "adidas" headband during games. Jim responded by wearing the first "Rozelle" headband. I felt then as I feel now that it was a disrespectful thing to do. But I probably should have kept my opinion to myself.

Jim's only response was to point out my punt against the Bears. He said, "I don't comment on guys who kick a ball one yard." OK, an eye for an eye.

The bottom line on my feelings about Jim is yes, he is "cocky, and a little bit of hot dog," to use his own words. But he is also a winner. I hope he can come back and play. The game and the Bears need him.

Gene Stallings, the Cardinals' coach, once said: "You run 70 plays in a football game, and 65 of them are to beat each other around. In that game there will be five occasions when somebody can make a play that will decide who wins." Of those five plays, chances are the quarterback will be in on three or four of them. He'll make something out of nothing. Maybe he'll throw a rocket downfield. Or he'll scramble loose and make a big play. Great teams with good quarterbacks are not as likely to win championships as good teams with great quarterbacks.

The perfect quarterback? Take Terry Bradshaw's arm, John Elway's athletic ability, for pure strength. For touch, Dan Fouts's tenacity, and Bob Griese's alertness. A talent for improvisation? Joe Montana. For play action, Kenny Stabler. Confidence, Roger Staubach.

Take all those guys and obviously, the composite would be the best. But the man at the top of my list is Joe Montana.

If quarterbacking were gunfighting, there were three years—'82, '83, '84—when I'd have put my gun up against anybody. I wouldn't have been afraid to walk out of a saloon knowing that any one of those guys was out there waiting to try me. Before those years, though, I'd have probably stayed in the bar with ol' Whiskey and Riggo.

The thing I wanted most was to become the best ballhandling quarterback. Sure, a quarterback has to be able to throw. But hiding and faking, that was the real challenge. Joe Montana is so good at it that sometimes you say, "Where is the ball?" The great ones can amaze you every time.

Terry Bradshaw could throw fire, like Elway and Dan Marino today, only harder. He also had great confidence, because he knew that no matter what he did mechanically, if he threw four interceptions, the Steelers still were going to win. A lot of that came because he had great receivers in Lynn Swann and John Stallworth who could catch anything . . . in a crowd, over the middle, deep, anywhere. All Terry had to do was get the ball in their vicinity.

Same thing with Dan Fouts, who had John Jefferson and Charlie Joiner and Kellen Winslow. Sometimes Terry and Dan could simply ignore the defense and just throw. It's not that they didn't recognize the defense. They just looked past it and threw toward those receivers wherever they were.

Knowing the abilities of your receivers is as important as knowing the defense. Fouts and Bradshaw proved that. How many times have you seen Stallworth or Jefferson come down in a crowd with the football? Basically, the football should never be thrown into a crowd—period. You're supposed to go to the receiver who's open or is being covered by one man.

So, in theory, you should never see the receiver fighting two defenders for a ball. But you'd see Bradshaw throwing it anywhere and it didn't matter, because Swannie would come down with it.

You have to know your receivers. You have to build confidence in receivers, let them know that you're going to get them the ball and you're going to take care of them. You do that by taking a young receiver aside and saying, "Look, don't be afraid to go over the middle, I'll protect you, I won't string you out." You don't want him to have to expose his ribs. You keep it low or try to hit him in the hands around the chest or waist. If all else fails, you let him dive for it.

Of course, you still have those receivers with what we call "alligator arms." You ever see an alligator's arms? No extension. Some receivers won't stick their arms out to catch a pass. But then you take guys like Stallworth or Swann and they'll go up like the greatest trapeze artists in the world to get a pass.

So you've got your alligators and your Wallendas, and it's the quarterback's job to know which is which.

I used to study Dan Fouts on film when Joe Gibbs first came to the Redskins. Dan is limited physically, as far as foot speed and strength go, but he has an extremely quick release, great timing, and is a great leader. It is amazing to watch Dan throw the ball. I'd think, "If I ever tried to throw to those people in those areas, I'd be out of work tomorrow." But Dan's passes would turn into touchdowns because of his timing and because he knew his receivers could beat their defenders.

I could never be that kind of quarterback. I didn't have the big gun and I didn't have the receiving corps. I tried to measure myself by the standards of Bob Griese and Joe Montana, great ballhandlers with great mobility who read defenses quickly, understood their team's system, and made good decisions about where to throw the ball. Joe is extremely dangerous when you get him out of the pocket and give him a chance to improvise. You get Joe running around, and nine times out of ten, something good is going to happen for the 49ers. I was mobile, but a notch below Montana, and I tended to run around without looking down the field. Not only can Montana move around, he picks out people down the field and gets the ball to them. His mobility is the best, his play-action faking is the best, and he's best at running his team's offense. Among quarterbacks, he's at the top of the mountain.

All of these qualities, the arm, the timing, the intelligence, the improvisation—all of it means nothing if you don't believe. I watched Billy Kilmer go out on that football field when he was lucky to be walking. He couldn't throw a spiral and he couldn't move very well. But that sucker believed he was the best. He could ignite his football team. He'd get in people's faces and chew them out. It worked for him, but it never would have worked for me. We were different personalities.

What Billy and I had in common was that we would never come out of games (unless, say, there was a broken leg involved). Sonny Jurgensen played hurt, Billy played hurt, I played hurt, Jay Schroeder plays hurt. It's a legacy of Redskin quarterbacks that I'm proud to have been a part of.

Every quarterback has to have that flaming desire to win. Jim McMahon shows he's ready by butting heads with his offensive linemen. Kenny Stabler had the swagger. For Kenny, instead of the skull and crossbones on the Raider helmet, they should have had a pirate with his sword in the air, one foot up on a cannon, captain of his warship.

Jack London, the writer who specialized in adventure stories, once wrote: "I would rather be ashes than dust. I would rather that my spark should burn out in a brilliant blaze than it should be stifled by dry rot. I would rather be a superb meteor than a sleepy, permanent planet."

Someone asked Kenny Stabler what London meant by that. "Throw deep," Kenny said.

10
Zip, Zoom, Zing, Zang ... Life with Joe Gibbs

I n the fall of 1980, there came over me the urge to dump hair lightener on my brown hair, turning it a blondish orange color. At the annual Welcome Home luncheon after training camp, Mr. Cooke said, "One day Joe looked like a Notre Dame quarterback, and the next day he looks like Mary Pickford. I don't know whether to give him a football or ask him to dance."

As far as I know, Mary Pickford never had her nose broken seven times, but I got the message. Mr. Cooke was not alone in wondering which Joe Theismann would show up. There was Joe the quarterback, Joe the businessman, Joe the pitchman. Somewhere there was even Joe Theismann the human being, though he wasn't around much.

In 1981 the Redskins seemed anxious to get rid of all those Joes. They drafted a quarterback in the fourth round, Tom Flick, out of the University of Washington. Some people were convinced that a trade was set with Detroit, me for Eric Hipple. Then Eric had a big game on Monday night TV and the deal was dead.

I have a letter dated February 3, 1982, confirming that Bobby Beathard talked to the Bears about a trade. Bears boss Jim Finks wrote to my agent, Ed Keating: "For your information, we had a discussion last fall with Bobby Beathard, instigated by Bobby, about a trade for Joe. Although our team was in a slump at the time and our quarterback was having a tough go of it, we decided that making a trade for Joe was not in our best long-range interests."

The Bears' long-range preference turned out to be the drafting of Jim McMahon, and though Jim and I have had our differences, you can't argue about his value to the Bears.

What I learned from all of this is that a pro athlete must, for sanity's sake, realize he is a replaceable part. They'll go to the quarterback store and get a new one, so don't get too comfortable. Still, it hurts to find out your team wants to trade you. I had begged George Allen to kick me out of his nursing home. But in 1981, it was different. I wanted to stay in Washington forever.

Even without Joe Walton on the staff in '81, I was excited, because Jack Pardee's successor, Joe Gibbs, was going to be my first offensive-minded head coach since Ara Parseghian at Notre Dame.

My path had actually crossed Joe's during my Notre Dame years. He was the offensive-line coach at Southern California under John McKay in 1969 and '70. Joe came into the NFL to work for his old college coach, Don Coryell, then the St. Louis Cardinals' coach. After five years with the Cardinals, he went to Tampa Bay with McKay again. That job lasted only a year. So Joe rejoined Coryell, this time with the San Diego Chargers.

That's where he was in 1980, largely anonymous, just another offensive coordinator whose biggest claim to fame was winning the 35-and-over national racquetball championship. Then Bobby Beathard got in touch with him. Bobby wanted Gibbs as his new man in charge. If Jack Kent Cooke had any doubts about Bobby's value as a football man, they should have been dispelled by Bobby's work in spotting Joe Gibbs as head coach material.

Joe hadn't been an NFL player. He was not a big name. He didn't even look like an NFL coach. No Don Shula granite jaw. None of Tom Landry's stern look of genius. Joe Gibbs looks like your eighth-grade science teacher. But as Bobby moved around the country on his decade of football scouting trips, first for Atlanta, then Miami, and later the Redskins, he kept up with Joe Gibbs's work and asked what other people thought of Joe.

"Everybody acted like Joe's press agent," Beathard said later. "Finally, I got to asking things like, 'How does he handle himself at the blackboard?' After a while, everything just reinforced itself in my mind that he'd be a good coach."

For a quarterback, the Joe Gibbs offense was a Christmas present that I couldn't wait to open. So what happened? We lost our first five games. It was bizarre because in those games I led all NFL quarterbacks in everything: completions, yards, touchdowns—and interceptions and losses. Somehow I had opened the Christmas present and put the toy together backward. The Hipple rumors started and the scuttlebutt started to make sense.

Beathard had won a power struggle to get Mr. Cooke to fire Pardee. He also sold Mr. Cooke on Joe Gibbs. It figured that an ambitious, powerful general manager might want his own quarterback instead of one brought in by the previous regime.

To make things worse, Joe Gibbs wasn't sold on Joe Theismann as his quarterback. Somebody had put a bug in his ear that football was secondary to my business interests, and that all I cared about was myself. "You've got to get rid of him if you want to win," they said. Not one to make snap judgments, he decided to give me a chance.

If you want to be a coach, the workaholic habits of a George Allen and a Joe Gibbs could change your mind. Three nights a week, Monday, Tuesday, and Wednesday, Joe slept on a sofa in his office at our training facility, Redskin Park. He wouldn't sleep at home until Thursday. Some weeks he went home on Sunday nights, some weeks he didn't. You do that 16 weeks a year, after doing it in training camp for a month, you become a zombie. Sometimes it seemed Joe would go through a whole practice session on a Friday without the faintest idea what he'd said. He couldn't function to his full mental capacity because he was so completely tired.

Now, if he just wanted to burn himself out, that's fine. But it was the coaching staff, too. You can't coach with Joe Gibbs unless you're willing to stay until three or four o'clock in the morning four days a week. He nearly killed his offensive coordinator, Jerry Rhome. In Jerry's first season, he aged ten years. He looked like the wrath of God had struck him down. Our backfield coach, Don Breaux, would fall asleep on the floor trying to grab 15 minutes of rest between meetings. We'd break for lunch and you'd see coaches' bodies all over the place.

To get ready for Dallas, they'd look at our two games of the previous season with them as well as the Cowboys' three or four most recent games. If the coaches spotted one particular defense—one way the Cowboys lined up that was different from all their other sets—Joe and the coaches might study that one strange defense for hours. And that defense might be a *mistake*. Or Randy White might have had a wild idea and lined up outside the end just to screw up everybody's life when they saw the film. Whatever the case, nothing was left to chance.

Our coaches were geniuses, no doubt about it, but they took it to a fanatical degree. They'd sit in meetings for hours dreaming up new "Z" words to use in our play calls. "Zip," "Zoom," "Zing," "Zang." We used colors to signal certain formations and they'd debate for hours whether "brown" might sound like "blue" when I called it out. If you ask me, this is taking attention to detail much too far. Dick Vermeil fried his cookies worrying about that stuff, and I began to kid Coach Gibbs about it. "How's it going, Dick?" I would say. Joe has acknowledged that he's worried about it, but knowing it and changing it are two different things.

It's debatable how long Joe can continue at that pace, because you can't push yourself that hard forever. There's no way he can be effective for 25 years. He'll be lucky to last ten years without paying some heavy price along the way, and that's too bad because Joe Gibbs belongs in a photo with Vince Lombardi and Don Shula and Tom Landry. He's that good.

Joe, like all coaches, would get angry if anybody backed off in practice. In the huddle, I'd say: "Look, the old man is over there and he's really getting agitated. I'm starting to see his glasses fog up. We're four plays into practice. If we don't start working, he's going to get real upset." We hated to see him mad because Joe didn't get mad that often, but when he did, you didn't want to be near him.

He especially didn't want you spouting off in the newspaper. Joe wanted his football team to be noncontroversial. Once, we had Dallas coming to Washington, and Dexter Manley popped off. Manley is a defensive end who is 6'3", 250, and very talented. One of our scouts, Mike Allman, liked Manley so much as a rookie that he said, "Ol' Dexter's gonna be great when he learns the difference between 'Come here' and 'Sic 'em.' " As Dexter's self-appointed media advisor for a while, I tried to help him. Small wonder, then, that Joe Gibbs picked up the paper and saw Dexter saying something like: "The Cowboys? Are they still in the league?"

This made Joe so furious that during the team meeting he took his fist and shattered the top of an overhead projector. We sat there in silence. Everyone stayed real quiet. Dexter, especially.

I played for Joe Gibbs for five years, winning one Super Bowl and going to another, and he still remains a mystery to me. Our relationship was often distant and unsettling. What we accomplished was very businesslike because we knew, as coach and quarterback, how important it was to share thoughts and feelings about our work. Even that took a while, and the turning point came at 0-5 in Joe's first season.

Joe tried to be a warm, decent man. But this was the cold, cruel National Football League, and there was a certain chill between Joe and me. He never said anything about it and, in fact, later denied to me that it ever existed. But I felt it, and it felt exactly like what I'd gone through with Billy Kilmer in quarterback meetings. Now it was happening again, only this time it was worse because it was the head coach making me feel like a fifth wheel. It wasn't that Joe didn't say anything to me; it was something in his attitude that made me uneasy, like he was the coach stuck with a quarterback he didn't want, didn't trust, and was planning to dump as soon as he could. If the handwriting were on the wall of our meeting room, it would have said, "Theismann, you're just passing through." There was a wall of suspicion and doubt between Joe Gibbs and me that was particularly scary, coming as it did after my wonderful years of give-and-take with Joe Walton. I felt my job growing more and more in jeopardy. During our fifth straight loss in '81, Gibbs benched me and put in Tom Flick.

It doesn't matter if you're Johnny Unitas, Bart Starr, or Joe Namath, if a team loses five games in a row, the coach is going to wonder about his quarterback. He might even change quarterbacks permanently. There's not much reason to stick with a loser. The season is shot so he might as well take a look at a new guy. Whatever the truth was in '81, I felt I was one game away from the end of my Redskin career.

Joe was under pressure, too, as a rookie head coach starting off 0-5. Reporters asked him if he expected to be fired. I guess we both were on the hot seat, and, in retrospect, it makes sense to think Joe's coolness toward me might have been nothing but a case of rookie-coach nerves and inexperience. He had every right, with his job on the line, to be wondering whether I cared enough about football to be the respected player a team needs at quarterback.

So I knocked on his door at home the night of our fifth-straight loss to tell him I was precisely that kind of player.

It was October 4, 1981. That afternoon we had lost to San Francisco, 31–14. We were going nowhere. I had been benched. Once upon a time, I went to George Allen's house out of fear he'd shoot me dead for running my mouth in the newspaper. This time I went to Joe's house out of the greater fear that he wouldn't let me play anymore. I didn't know how Joe would react to me showing up at his house and rousting him out of bed. He might tell me to get lost. He might say he was going to trade me to Buffalo. If he had told me the worst thing imaginable—let's say Tom Flick would be the starter from then on—it made no difference. I had to find out what he was thinking and it couldn't wait.

It was 9 o'clock, pitch dark, when I pulled into his driveway. I took a deep breath, got out of the car, and slowly walked to the door. I knocked, half hoping he wouldn't be there. I had never been very good at confrontation. I would rather wait for something to happen, and deal with the results.

Fortunately, though, his wife Pat answered the door and invited me in.

We sat in the living room, facing each other. It was very uncomfortable and very hard to do, but I had to do it because I was fighting for my life. Football defined me, it thrilled me, it made me feel like somebody. Without football, I couldn't exist. And I couldn't play football this way. You can't go on the field thinking you'll be replaced if you mess up a pass.

The meeting was between him and me as people, not as head coach and quarterback. I went to his house trying to find an answer from a man, not from my boss.

"I get the feeling that something's not right between us," I said. "Something's missing. I sit in meetings, you're the coach, I'm the player, and that's about where it stops. I'm smart enough to know that we've got to be closer if this thing's going to have a chance to work."

I tried in a not very effective way to describe how uncomfortable the quarterback meetings were, how I felt I was on the outside looking in, not really a part of anything.

Joe said he didn't understand. I told him: "There's something you don't know, Joe, and that's how committed Joe Theismann is to the game of football. I want to play. I want to run your system. But something's just not right. Listen, Joe, football is No. 1 to me."

He said: "I want a quarterback I can call up in the summer to come in and work out a receiver. I don't want some guy who's off on a business deal."

"You never tried me," I said. "I'll do that. I'm willing. That's the kind of sacrifice and work commitment I'm willing to make. I've done it all my life. Give me a chance, Joe. Somebody's sold you a bill of goods on me, and I want you to know that whatever they've said, I'm here to play football."

"Nobody said anything to me about you," Joe said.

Well, OK. I didn't believe it, but I wouldn't harp on it. At last, Joe Gibbs understood me. He knew something he didn't know before. Maybe I wouldn't sleep on the office floor at four in the morning, but now Joe knew football had the same priority in my life as in his. Joe Theismann was first, last, and always a football player.

We hadn't won a game five Sundays into the season when I knocked on Joe's door that night. When I left his house, we were on our way to the Super Bowl.

11
And the Crowd
Goes Wild

After my midnight meeting with Joe Gibbs, we won eight of our last 11 games in his rookie season. When we lost all four preseason games in '82, a *Washington Post* columnist wrote, "The Redskins are five years away from a Super Bowl." You know, maybe George Atkinson had it right. The old Raider defensive back once was asked what players would do if the press box blew up. "We'd have 30 seconds of respectful silence," George said, "and then continue with enthusiasm."

The *Post*'s writer was wrong—by five years. We won the whole thing in '82 because, when we were 0-5 the year before, Joe Gibbs was brave enough to ditch his San Diego–style offense. I wasn't Dan Fouts and we weren't the Chargers. We went to a one-back offense with John Riggins running and me throwing from behind our big linemen, the Hogs. Our guys also played hellacious defense, and, as in George Allen's time, our special teams were sensational.

Our first victory for Joe Gibbs came in Chicago. Neal

Olkewicz returned an interception for a touchdown. Dave Butz also intercepted one, and we recovered a fumble at the one-yard line. With that defensive work, we won 24–7. It was more than just a victory. There's a thin line between winning and losing. Once you learn to win—or to lose— it's contagious.

We caught the immortality bug. The Chicago victory began an era in which we won 41 of 50 games. We won a Super Bowl, lost a Super Bowl, and reached the playoffs three consecutive years for the first time in a decade. Lombardi's Packers of the mid-'60s, Shula's Dolphins of the early '70s, and Noll's Steelers of the mid-'70s were the last teams to be so dominant. Nice company for the Redskins.

Our opener in '82 set the tone for an unforgettable year. Philadelphia had us down, 34–24, with about five minutes left. But then Charlie Brown caught an 80-yard touchdown pass, and we came back with some great catches by Art Monk to tie it on Mark Moseley's 48-yard field goal as time ran out. Mark won it with a 26-yarder in overtime.

All season we found a way to win, mostly with defense and Mark's phenomenal kicking. He ran a streak of successive field goals to 23, an NFL record. He was 20-for-21 for the year, an accuracy record. He became the only kicker ever named the league's MVP and Mark earned it. IF he'd had a kicker's normal year, we'd have been 5–4. With a great year, maybe 7–2. Instead, we were 8–1. There has never been a better kicker under pressure. Mark won 17 games in his Washington career by kicking field goals in the last four minutes.

This was also the strike season, 1982. The NFL lost seven regular-season games when the NFL Players Association called a strike after the first two games. Ed Garvey, the NFLPA's boss, said we were striking for 55 percent of all revenue. "Etched in stone," he said. He even had a piece of rock in his office with "55%" etched on it.

The NFLPA took such an antimanagement stance that it lost a real opportunity to help the players. We had a snowball's chance in hell of ever getting the owners to hand over 55 percent of their football income. We should have been striking for free agency and guaranteed contracts not some piece of a rock.

But Garvey and our union leaders said we had no shot at free agency, even though baseball players, basketball players, and hockey players have long had the right to sell their services on the open market. It was Garvey's contention that football owners would conspire and not bid for anyone, effectively defeating the concept of free agency. That view was more cynical than true, I think, because next to quarterbacks and coaches, owners have the biggest egos in the world. They want to win, and to win they'll pay the freight for the best players available.

We're talking boys and their toys. If one owner has a nice bicycle with a really neat horn—let's say that horn is a quarterback—another owner will want that horn because he thinks it'll make his bike the best bike on the block. He'll pay for that really neat horn.

But it can't happen that way. So the owners have fought to avoid free agency for players, not only to keep their best players but to make sure salaries don't escalate as they have in baseball and basketball. Players are locked in with no way out. They are the owner's property. If you're lucky, as I was with Mr. Cooke, the team owner will pay you handsomely for your work.

Unlike 1974, when I crossed the picket line of old Redskins and alienated everyone forever, in 1982 I didn't want any controversy. This time I became a more active leader than I ever had been. The six weeks we were on strike, I organized practices for the guys at a suburban park. It was the first time I had actually tried to assume a leadership role.

The best leaders are those players who do their jobs as well as they possibly can, and maybe a few times they somehow do better than anyone thought. You need to exude confidence. And how can a quarterback get 10 other guys to believe in him if he doesn't believe in himself? There's a fine line between "confident" and "cocky," and I should know.

I've pushed that line a few times. What it boils down to is belief in yourself, no matter what. Leadership can be the rah-rah stuff, fire in your eyes, grabbing a lineman by the face mask, butting somebody in the head. But it doesn't have to be.

My buddy Pete Wysocki, once tried to explain why I couldn't be the prototypical holler-guy leader. "In the offensive huddle, a word or two dominates the atmosphere," Pete said. "You don't have a lot of people talking. The quarterback talks and that's it.

"But with Joe, it was different. Joe just wasn't a screamer. Joe was Captain Bubbly, all effervescence and little-boy enthusiasm. Hey, you can't have Pinky Lee play Al Capone."

It isn't always the quarterback who leads. On our Super Bowl teams, George Starke was a leader. So were Tony McGee, John Riggins, and Art Monk. Look at Joe Jacoby, a free-agent tackle nobody wanted, a great guy who made himself into a great player. You're respected for the work you do, not for what you say. You *can* be Pinky Lee as long as you get Al Capone results.

A quarterback is always the first player questioned about leadership if his team loses. It's a bogus issue sportswriters dredge up. They forget the real reasons a team may lose. Such as, no talent or bad coaching. Somehow it does come down to "no leadership," and that usually falls on the quarterback even though he is the most dependent guy on the team. Unless the other 10 guys do their jobs well, the quarterback can't get his done. In '82, if Mark hadn't kicked all those field goals, we'd have had an ordinary record. But he hit 20 in a row and we won big. Mark, a kicker, a position that *real* football players won't even acknowledge as "real," led our team.

We won our first two games in '82 and then didn't play for almost two months while Ed Garvey slowly but surely gave up on his 55 percent. All the strike did was paint one more picture of pro athletes as spoiled, greedy children. Through it all, we only wanted to play football.

During the strike, we'd meet at a park for a practice from 10 until noon. We'd do calisthenics, go through passing drills, repeat plays from old game plans, make up plays, horse around. Sometimes we'd just play touch. I'd be wide receiver, defensive back, whatever. Some days we'd have eight guys, other days 25. The running backs, receivers, and defensive backs all stuck together. The linemen, those dear Hogs, went off to practice on their own. Probably somewhere with burgers and brew.

Those six weeks made up one of the most important periods of my life. Joe Gibbs may never have known about our workouts. Management wasn't supposed to be around. We were different kinds of people, Gibbs and I, but if he had any last doubts about my commitment to football, they should have been erased during the strike.

Those workouts were the reason we came back so strongly after the strike. People said, "The veteran teams will come out of this best because they're so used to each other that six weeks apart won't hurt them." We weren't a veteran team at all. We were a makeshift ball club thrown together by Bobby Beathard and Gibbs from free agents, trades, and low-round draft picks—all patched around a nucleus of old heads left over from George Allen's time.

But we came right out and beat the Giants at the Meadowlands, 27–17. The next four weeks were indicative of our future. We scored only 51 points and gave up 54, but we won three of the games with defense and Moseley's kicking. Unbelievable. When we started scoring, it was the creation of an offensive machine. We won our last two regular-season games, 27–10 and 28–0, before winning the first two playoff games, 31–7 and 21–7.

What goes around comes around. Ray Schoenke had told me to be patient with the Billy Kilmer situation. *You'll have your day,* he said. If it was small and mean of me to have enjoyed that moment in 1978 when I waved Kilmer off the field, there came a moment in 1983 when it was my day without question.

The playoff victories had put us in the NFC championship game. To get to the Super Bowl—the dream of my childhood, the dream of my life—all we had to do was win one more game.

That game would be against the Dallas Cowboys at RFK Stadium.

You leave football with wonderful memories of work shared with men who gave as much of themselves as you did. And if you're lucky, you get to play in one game like Washington-Dallas on January 22, 1983.

The White House closed its press office just before kickoff. At Lorton Reformatory, 1,237 inmates huddled around 25 TV sets. Richard Helms, the former director of the Central Intelligence Agency, sat in Jack Kent Cooke's box. Helms wore an Indian headdress.

Mr. Cooke told a reporter what it all meant. "Look at this," he said. This gentleman, worth about $600 million by a 1986 *Forbes* magazine estimate, swept a trembling hand around RFK. He said: "This is controlled delirium. There is a coagulation, a community of interest here that is astonishing in its depth. All over this city. The rich, the poor. The black, the white."

Mr. Cooke was only getting warmed up. He went on with rising passion.

"The communists, the socialists. The affluent, the dispossessed. All are bound together in this city on this day by these Redskins."

And we hadn't even kicked off yet.

In that football stadium that day, there were 55,045 lives made into one. The whole stadium was like a heart pounding. Wysocki said, "The place whirred, like it was a spaceship, humming like it was going to leave the Earth." You were inside this living thing that energized you, lifted you up, made you stronger than you'd ever been, faster than you'd ever been, maybe even smarter.

We were on fire. We were unstoppable. We were the Fun Bunch and the Smurfs and the Pearl Harbor Crew and the Bald Eagles and Riggo's Rangers. It was like the 15th round of a heavyweight fight, and we had the champion Cowboys on the ropes. They'd beaten us six straight times, and they never let us forget it. They never let us forget '79, when Roger Staubach got them two touchdowns in the last two minutes to win, 35–34. Their defensive tackle Randy White mouthed off every chance he got about what a bunch of crybabies the Redskins were, especially the quarterback Theismann.

The hot-dog quarterback completed 12 of 20 passes for 150 yards and a touchdown that day. They were all big plays, but one stands out. We led, 14–10, midway in the third quarter. It was third-and-18 from the Dallas 28. We rolled the pocket to the right, as we'd done hundreds of times, even thousands of times, in games and in practice and in the park during the strike. Some Cowboy was chasing me hard. On the run, I saw Charlie Brown downfield.

Firefox is a movie about a Russian jet fighter with guns that are aimed and fired by thought. The pilot sees something, the guns shoot it down. It was like that here: I remember seeing Charlie, but I don't remember throwing the ball. Somehow it got there. A 22-yard gain. First down. Two runs later, Riggins scored. It was 21–10 on the way to a 31–17 final.

I've never been more thrilled—or frightened—than I was standing on RFK's sidelines with the clock ticking down to the end of that game. People kept coming up to me, saying, "Congratulations." I shoved them away, screaming, "It's not over yet, it's not over."

People went insane. They came out of the stands to tear up the field, to tear down the goalposts. Literally, the ground shook. It trembled. You could feel it under your feet. And to stamp this day as unforgettable, we ran our last 10 plays directly at Randy White. Our linemen wanted it that way.

In the locker room afterward, I told anybody who would listen that it was the greatest moment of my life. "We beat the Cowboys, we're going to the Super Bowl. What else could you want?"

Well, you could want to win the Super Bowl by beating Don Shula and the Miami Dolphins the next week.

12
The Ultimate Game

The Goodyear blimp is overhead, planes are skywriting movie ads, a thousand balloons are released to float past the flags fluttering at the rim of the Rose Bowl. Blue-jeaned preachers get on bullhorns to say, "Jesus loves you sinners." Richard Nixon calls a talk show in Washington and says we are "the team from nowhere," meaning it as a compliment, meaning we rose up so quickly we caught everyone by surprise.

About the Super Bowl, Duane Thomas once said, "If it's the 'ultimate' game, why are they playing one next year?" Maybe Duane was right, but the way I felt, it sure was bigger than South River High against New Brunswick, and that's big.

If you're lucky, there is a moment in your life when everything comes together so neatly that it seems it was supposed to happen that way. I believe everything happens according to the Lord's plan and we couldn't change it if we tried. I'm not saying the Lord wanted the Redskins in the 1983 Super Bowl or that He wanted Joe Theismann to be the quarterback that day. But He gave us life and gave us the tools and the blueprint to do it. All we had to do was use them.

The first day of Super Bowl week in Pasadena, I told reporters: "As a kid in New Jersey, I wanted someday to be in Joe Namath's shoes or Johnny Unitas's or Bart Starr's. Now here I stand. Pinch me, I want to see if this is real."

The only moments of sanity during Super Bowl week are those in meetings and practices. Every day you do press conferences for the media from all over the world. A thousand sportswriters come to town. They bring their wives, they go to Disneyland, they go to fancy restaurants. They listen to players talk in the morning so they can write their stories in time to be on the first tee at noon for a golf tournament.

All those newspapermen. All those TV cameras. I never had so much fun.

Not to say I talked a lot that week, but here's one headline after a press conference: "Theismann wears out tape recorders." Another: "He's a mouthful, that Theismann." One fellow wrote, "To say that Theismann is cocky is to say Mozart wrote tunes." Another said, "If talking is an Olympic sport, Theismann is Jim Thorpe."

On Thursday of that crazy week, I knew we were on the right track. There came to Joe Gibbs's eye the little twinkle that tells us he's come up with a good idea and he knows it. The coaches called his brainstorm the "Explode Package," because when you drew it on paper it looked like the formations were exploding.

We would use the Explode Package inside Miami's 20-yard line. It was a series of four plays with the tight ends, wingbacks, wide receivers, and running backs all shifting from one position to a new one. The quarterback and the five Hogs stood still. Because Miami's defense matched up man-to-man inside the 20, Coach Gibbs felt they would have trouble finding the players they were supposed to cover if everybody else ran around like crazy. Joe said we might use the package even if we didn't get inside the 20, just to hear what the TV announcers would say.

One of Joe's great gifts is his ability to keep every week new and exciting. If you're playing football from July to December with the same ugly group of guys, it can get pretty stale. Repetition is the key to success in football, but repetition also can bore you to death. Gibbs kept our attention and made each week fun by coming up with new formations, new plays, and variations of old plays.

For instance, the "throw-back special" was designed to take advantage of the defense ganging up on John Riggins. Practically everything we did began by either handing the ball to John or faking it to him. The throw-back special began as a straight dive with Riggins, a play we'd used to gain hundreds of yards. But when Gibbs decided the defenses would be anticipating Riggins, he put in the variation: Riggins would spin and toss the ball back to me, and I would hit somebody deep downfield—unless, say, the pocket caved in and some Giants fell on my leg and it goes *Pow! Pow!*

So much had gone into the trip to Pasadena: South River, Notre Dame, the years in Canada, the wasted days with George Allen, the rocky beginnings with Joe Gibbs. I always felt the football fans in Washington disliked me. When Allen forced Sonny Jurgensen to retire in 1974, it seemed that a legend had been booted out to make room for this kid. Somehow I became a villain.

Then I competed with Billy and won the job from a guy who'd been a Washington monument of his own. Sonny and Billy were loved in Washington. They still are loved and they earned the right to be loved. They were great quarterbacks, and I'm proud to have been their successor. But I could never really replace them in the hearts of Washington football fans.

There was only one way, I thought, to get the fans to accept me. That was to go out and win a championship. Be the quarterback of a championship team. Sonny and Billy had never done that. I would. There I was—pinch me if I'm dreaming—on my way to the Super Bowl, riding in our team bus down the steep hills of suburban Pasadena toward a gigantic stadium in a valley ringed by mountains with snow on the peaks. '

Just writing about it gives me chills. Everything seems so clear, as if it's happening again. I can see the locker room in the Rose Bowl. It doesn't even have a locker. All I got was a metal folding chair and a nail in the wall. This is the Super Bowl and I'm hanging my clothes on a nail. But it makes no difference on this day because this locker room, like all winning locker rooms, feels good.

Just as you come out of the locker room tunnel at the end zone, the field is damp. It's a clear day, a little misty. It would turn into a dreamy fog later. It's my habit, a routine, a superstition maybe, to walk from end zone to end zone before a game. No stopping at the 50-yard line. Stopping at all means that's as far as I'll get in the game. So I walked from end to end. Now I've been on every piece of the turf. It's my turf now.

We're here two hours early. I haven't shaved. I never shaved on game day. Time to get down and dirty. We sit around and talk. No one's nervous. It's early. The night before, Joe Gibbs said: "Guys, you've got to put up with me. I've got some things I have to say." He began every talk that way. Joe said we'd accomplished a lot, and for some people that might be enough. "But there are other people who want to be great," Joe said. "And tomorrow is going to be our chance to be great."

Rockne couldn't have done better. The morning of the game, I was at breakfast with tackle George Starke, quarterback Tommy Owen, and John Riggins. John said, "I think I'm going to carry the ball about 40 times and run for about 200 yards."

"That'd be OK with me, J.R.," I said.

Earlier in the week, John had gone to Don Breaux, the backfield coach, and asked, "What's the Super Bowl rushing record?" It was 158 yards. Don didn't know the number, but he was impressed that John was confident enough to ask.

Now we're in the Rose Bowl locker room two hours before kickoff. Every player has his routine to get ready. Mine was always the same. Each piece of clothing comes off in precisely the same order and each piece of my uniform goes on in precisely the same order. My socks are tucked into the right side of my jock. I've got some time to kill because I'll be the last guy to get taped. I stack some towels on the floor for a pillow, prop my feet up on a chair, and read *People* magazine. Every article. Every word. From beginning to end. An incomplete article is an incomplete thought is an incomplete pass.

For a few minutes, I'll doze off next to my game plan. I'm through with the game plan. If I don't know it by now, I'm in serious trouble. But I keep it close, just in case. Around the room, I see backfield coach Don Breaux going over signals with the other quarterbacks. We don't need it by now, but it makes Don feel better.

Our line coach, Joe Bugel, is at the blackboard, X'ing and O'ing. Everyone is real comfortable. There is an air about our people. They know they're good. They've proved it. Of course, this doesn't stop them from walking to the bathroom a lot. Every time they go in there, they see the big photo of the 49ers' Super Bowl ring from the year before. Our trainer, Bubba Tyer, pasted it up there. We're getting wired. Voices go lower. Not many words now. An occasional shout, "ALL RIGHT!"

A half hour to go. I've taped my toes, the big toes, and the balls of my feet. Only Bubba tapes my ankles. In my 12 years with the Redskins, only Bubba taped me. Always my right ankle first. Now I'm switching back and forth from *People* to my game plan.

Back at my locker, I put the pads in my pants. First the left knee, then the right. The left thigh pad and then the right. I stick hip pads inside my jock and tape them down. This is war. We're talking combat gear. I put my pants on, put on a T-shirt with a V-cut in the neck, pull my shoulder pads over my head, and tie everything down.

And I don't want anyone helping me. Leave me alone.

Don't help me even if my jersey is stuck on a pad. I can do it. I'll stretch it until it's loose, and I'll tuck it into my pants. No loose ends, no strings hanging out, nothing untied.

I always take my helmet, check the cheek pads, spin the helmet around one time like you'd spin six-shooters, and put it on. Then, as I leave the locker room, the last man out, I reach up with my left hand and touch the Redskin logo taped over the doorway by our equipment man.

It was time to go do it. We walked through the dark tunnel and into the sunlight, out of the privacy of our thoughts into the public clamor around our actions. I always loved running onto a football field. I did it first in South River, later at Notre Dame and at RFK, and now I was running onto a Super Bowl field, the dream made real. I don't remember my feet touching the ground.

We started the game with 50 Gut. That's a run off left tackle by John. Our last running play would be 50 Gut. And we would run it two dozen times in between. "We thought we could run on Miami," our center Jeff Bostic would say, "and by the end of the third quarter we knew it for sure. They weren't getting as excited and not as many guys were helping out on tackles. It was ours."

If you're the quarterback in this situation, you give the ball to your big blaster behind your big Hogs on the left side: Joe Jacoby, Russ Grimm, and Bostic. Then you stand there and admire their work.

To get to that situation, though, we had to survive a scary moment in the third quarter. Miami was leading, 17–13, and had us backed up inside our 20-yard line. I went back to pass. On my right, no one was open. Back to the left, I saw Charlie Brown and hurried a pass his way.

Kim Bokamper, Miami's defensive end, deflected the ball. It popped straight up and I lost sight of it. Everything went to slow motion, like in a car wreck, where your concentration is so intense everything seems to happen slowly. Then I saw the ball. And Bokamper was running under it, like a receiver, near our goal line, and it would be a touchdown!

It would be 24-13, Miami, and we'd have just over a quarter to catch up.

Better do something. Better get to the ball before Bokamper does. But my legs were stuck in cement. It was like a nightmare. Couldn't move. Couldn't get there. Finally, I just dove, trying to anticipate where the ball would be and get myself close enough to bat it away. I ripped my hand across Bokamper's arms and somehow knocked the ball loose.

Of all my passes that year, of all the plays we ran, that's the one I remember most. So it was still 17-13 when we later came to the play that won the game for us.

We had fourth down, one yard to go, on Miami's 43-yard line with about 10 minutes to play. There was no question what we would do. We had to go for the first down. And if we did that, we'd run it. And if we ran it, we'd run John Riggins behind our left side. No secrets here. Here comes 70 Chip, a play with a blocker leading Riggins to left tackle.

Everyone knew what we would do. So I considered doing what no one expected. I thought about faking the ball to John and keeping it myself on a naked bootleg around the right end. I would run in for the touchdown and become the Super Bowl hero.

It made sense in a bizarre and borderline-lunatic way. We had run so many similar plays with John that the fake surely would fool everybody. I seriously considered it. To admit this in public is, of course, to admit that on that day, at that moment, I seriously needed my head examined.

I came to my senses and thought, "This is one of those times in your life when you're losing, it's fourth-and-one, and if John has a hole to run through while you get trapped with the ball, they're going to kill you."

By "they," I meant my own guys.

They would have killed me.

And no court in the land would have convicted them. It would have been justifiable quarterbackicide.

A voice said: "Don't even entertain this thought anymore. Give the ball to John."

He took it. He moved up behind a blocker. He got the first down and then—holy shit!—he was going for a touchdown. He burst through tackle, cut to his left, wriggled out of Don McNeal's tackle, and outran every Dolphin to the end zone. Now we led, 20–17, and a few minutes later, on my second touchdown pass, this one to Charlie Brown, we made it 27–17. That was the final score.

And I got to call the game's last play. John had carried 38 times for 166 yards. I had completed 15 of 23 passes for 143 yards. Now we ran out the clock, which meant I took the snap and knelt down with the ball. The usual call was "save-the-game formation." For this it was "winning Super Bowl formation on Red."

Of the millions of words that have passed these lips, few ever were sweeter.

Joe Gibbs would say about winning the Super Bowl: "A lot of things go through your mind. I was thanking the Lord and I was thinking back to how many hours and how much work had gone into this day. So many hope to be Super Bowl champs, and here we were, on the verge of fulfilling that dream. It was kind of overwhelming."

President Reagan called our locker room and told Joe Gibbs, "It was just great." Riggo shouted out, "At least for tonight, Ron's the president, but I'm king."

I was the happiest man on the face of the earth. It's more than just the winning. The winning is only the icing on the cake. It's a team game, and you get a feeling of camaraderie with your teammates. You've been through the hell of training camp. You've been through six weeks of a strike. You've worked so hard to win close games. Somehow you won games you weren't supposed to win. Guys played bigger than they were, they played better than they were. There is in fact a sweet spot in time when it all comes together as if it were meant to be.

A lifetime of work moves you to that moment. You tack up Johnny Unitas's picture on your bedroom wall. You play ball every day. You go to Canada before winding up on somebody's bench in the NFL for five years. And then you get to a Super Bowl. It was only one football season, and it was only one game. But it took a lifetime.

13
Riggo and Me

John Riggins usually wore blue jeans and cowboy boots, the working man's clothes, just right for a Hog. Our tackle George Starke once said: "John is a living representation of an old Hank Williams, Jr., song. 'Hard drinkin', hard fightin', ornery.' "

To which John said, "Fightin'? No, I'm not a fighter."

John liked being one of the Hogs even if he wasn't a lineman. "A fullback," he said, "ain't nothin' but a guard who got lost on the way to the line of scrimmage."

On the Friday night before our first Super Bowl game, Mr. Cooke threw a party for the team, and John came in smiling, fashionably late, wearing a top hat, tails, and white gloves. He carried a beer in his right hand.

Only J.R. had the charisma to pull off this wonderful piece of theater. He was Bronko Nagurski in Fred Astaire's tux. When someone asked if he intended to dance on the tables, John said, "Not yet. But the evening is young."

Our Redskins were a circus with a tent full of acts never before seen on this continent. We had the famous Hogs, our offensive line, rooting out yardage. The center, Jeff Bostic, said: "Being called a Hog is appropriate. We're always doing a lot of work on the ground, in the mud, just like hogs. Besides, this makes us different from everyone else on the team. It's something to joke about. It's still a kid's game, and when you can't laugh, you better get out."

We had the Smurfs, our little receivers, and we had the Fun Bunch, who celebrated with leaping high-fives in the end zone. Our secondary people called themselves the Pearl Harbor Crew because everyone tried to bomb them. We had the Bald Eagles, our linebackers, short on hair but long on meanness.

All we needed at Mr. Cooke's party was a ringmaster to say, "Ladies and gentlemen, boys and girls of all ages, presenting now for your fascination and entertainment, in the center ring, the one and only hog who wears top hat and tails, Mr. John Riggins."

What an athlete John was. Dedicated, driven, tremendously strong, tremendously resistant to pain, well above-average speed, well above-average hands. One of the best football players ever. He had such a great set of haunches on him. His ass and legs were so powerful that when he ran, you could see the muscles ripple. You could literally see the power. He was 240 pounds and he was fast. There wasn't a tackler born who wanted to meet John Riggins head-on.

John and I never ran in the same crowd, and it's right to say we knew each other best in the literal passing of a football from my hands to his. Yet a hundred threads bound us together, threads of teamwork, of attention, of dedication. We also had our problems. John drank. I gambled. And we both overdid it.

A beer or two after practice was such a Redskin tradition that we had a "Five O'Clock Club" even in the late '60s, when Vince Lombardi coached the team in the last year of his life. The original Five O'Clock Club had been in a Victorian frame house across the street from the training-camp dorm in Carlisle. Lombardi would sit on the porch

Hard to believe this kid would one day make a movie with
Burt Reynolds.

My sister Patty couldn't lift a bat (even when I told her to choke up) . . . so I made a kicker out of her. She was no threat to Moseley.

Yes, I am weightlifting in the kitchen. No, this is not necessarily the way to become an NFL quarterback.

REPORT ON SCHOLARSHIP AND CITIZENSHIP

	FIRST QUARTER	SECOND QUARTER	THIRD QUARTER	FOURTH QUARTER
SCHOLARSHIP Is doing especially good work in	Number Work Spelling	Number Work Spelling	Number Work Spelling	Number Work Spelling
Is doing satisfactory work in	Reading Penmanship	Reading - Penmanship	Reading - is showing good progress Penmanship	Reading Penmanship
Is not doing satisfactory work in				
CITIZENSHIP	Talkative	Shows improvement	Is inattentive at times.	Tries to do his best in school.
Needs to give special attention to	Reading -	Needs lots of practice in oral and silent reading.		Reading- should read a little each day for practice.

My third grade report card: the teacher thought I was too talkative, and this was *before* I took Speech and Argumentation.

I loved baseball, until I heard about
Joe Namath and his llama-skin rug.

If Notre Dame had ever seen this
picture, what are the chances they
would have recruited me?

I had never even heard of Knute Rockne, and suddenly I'm playing for the Ghosts of the Golden Dome.

Ara Parseghian, larger than life, always in control. I was scared to death of him.

I gave up Don Shula and three Super Bowls to play in Toronto for Leo Cahill and a ferris wheel.

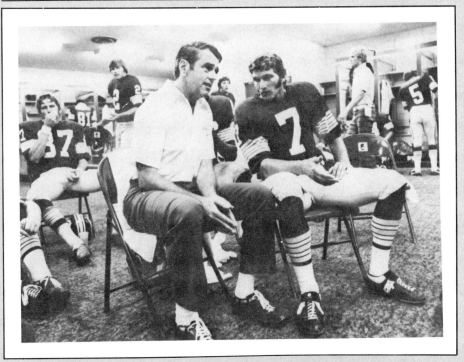

George Allen told me a dozen reasons why I was the perfect Redskin quarterback. Then he sat me on the bench for three years.

Mark Moseley took a lot of abuse for being a kicker as opposed to a "real" football player, but no one was more "real" than Mark when it came to those last-second field goals.

You have to know your receiver and pray that he isn't an "alligator." Ever see an alligator's arms? No extension.

I knew we were in trouble when this pass was intercepted by a duck.

When Drew Pearson and I played together at South River High School, we had no idea we'd end up on opposite sides of football's toughest rivalry.

Considering Tom Landry spent at least two Sundays each season trying to make my life miserable, we made quite a pair of allies in the Pro Bowl.

Joe Walton, our offensive coordinator in 1978 and today the head coach of the New York Jets, saved me from becoming the best clipboard holder in the league; he made me into a quarterback.

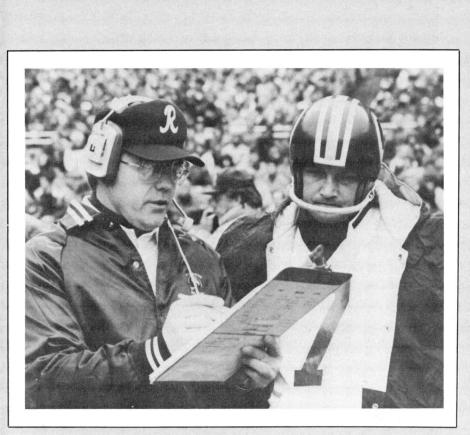
Joe Gibbs and I were as close as a coach and quarterback can be, but I'll never get over the hurt of being told by him that I couldn't stand on the sidelines with my broken leg.

That's golfer Tom Watson, just asking me for a few tips.

Words can't express how honored I was to be invited to dinner at the White House.

John Riggins always considered himself a Hog even though he wasn't a lineman. "A fullback," he said, "ain't nothin' but a guard who got lost on his way to the line of scrimmage."

John and I never ran in the same crowd, and despite the smiling faces here, we each had our problems. John drank. I gambled. Too much.

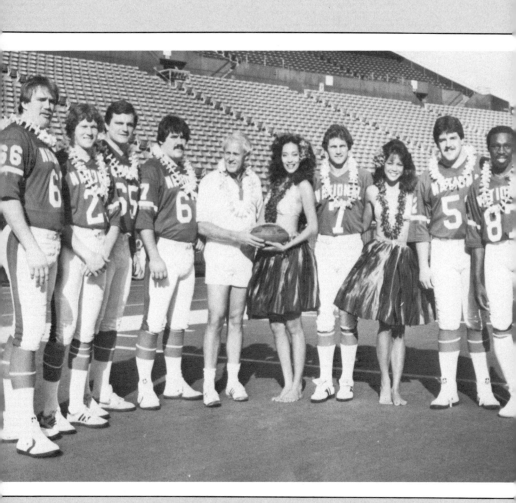

Some of the 1984 NFL Pro Bowl team—plus a couple of ringers we brought in.

A serious moment with the Theismanns: Joey, Amy, and
Patrick (below).

My family:
they'll never know
how much they mean to me.

Cathy Lee Crosby, the love of my life.

to have a drink with coaches and visitors.

In our generation, the Five O'Clock Club became a society of players who convened in a little red equipment shed just outside the locker room, at Redskin Park. The shed wasn't big enough for more than four or five guys. Some guys would stop by for one beer on the way home. Others would go in and come out a lot worse.

Joe Gibbs finally cut off all drinking on the premises. But he didn't do it until 1986, after we struggled in 1985. As long as you're winning, you can get away with most anything. But as soon as you start losing, the first thing the coaches do is clamp down on the players.

Still, they needed to do it. I drank my share of beverages a few years ago. I'd go to practice hung over and wonder why I did it to myself. My teeth hurt. Every little noise hurt my head, particularly the infernal racket of my hair growing.

I cut out that nonsense because I couldn't survive that way. With certain guys in Washington—Sonny Jurgensen, Billy Kilmer, John Riggins—it was all you heard about. Sonny once said, "All the bartenders in Philadelphia wore black armbands the day I was traded to Washington." Billy said: "I drink a lot. I drink what Sonny spills." Fans seemed to talk about their drinking as much as they talked about their exploits on the football field. And that's too bad because those guys ought to be thought of first for their great abilities. To go through the incredible hard work it takes to be a great quarterback or great running back only to be known as a drinker instead—it's a travesty and a waste.

At a Super Bowl press conference, someone asked John the secret to his longevity. "Formaldehyde," he said. Another time he said: "The only drinking problem I have is when I'm hanging from a rafter by my knees. Other than that, it goes down like everybody else."

Nobody from our Five O'Clock Club (members wore T-shirts) ever showed up for practice unable to perform, but with John there'd be days in the huddle when I didn't want to yell very loud. John was a Jekyll-and-Hyde character. When he was not into alcohol, he was a hell of a guy. But when he got to drinking, you just didn't know what he was going to do, as we found out in a sensational way in February 1985, when John went to a White House dinner and told Supreme Court Justice Sandra Day O'Connor, "Loosen up, Sandy baby."

Then the great fullback and Super Bowl MVP fell off his chair and slept 45 minutes through a speech by Vice President Bush. It was a disaster for John.

As much as cocaine is in the NFL news, alcohol is just as bad. We used to have a defensive lineman who'd sleep through team meetings, he was so drunk. To see people throw their career away for the bottle is sad.

The more I see of drug abuse, the more convinced I am that there's only one way to stop it. Pro athletes should submit to drug testing. The only way you'll ever reach them is through their pocket books. Unless testing becomes mandatory, with huge fines involved, the drug problem in sports isn't going to end. It may not be the ultimate solution, but it would be a start.

With the money available today, every team may have three or four coke users now. In the 1960s and '70s, athletes were more into performance-enhancing drugs than recreational drugs. But now the performance-enhancing drugs are under much tighter regulation. Besides, athletes are so much better trained they don't need chemical help. You look at them, coming out of those weight rooms, and they don't look human. In the '70s, we had Rocky Balboa, the human gladiator. The '80s brought us Ivan Drago, the technological machine created in the weight room.

Personally, I don't know how anybody survives football if they're very deep into alcohol or drugs. In Canada we had a "Dr. Feelgood" who passed through the locker room with his briefcase full of pills. We'd have guys so wired they'd bang their heads off walls or they'd wrap tape around their arms and beat the hell out of lockers. You'd see this vacant look in their eyes, like: "The elevator here does not go to the top floor. There is another human being inside this helmet. He eats small children for breakfast."

Both drugs and alcohol are so self-destructive they just don't make sense. Yet if you turned on the radio in the summer of '86, you could hear John Riggins doing a drive-time show, and all he did was make silly jokes about drinking. He sold himself short. He's a great guy with all the tools to be good at anything. There's a helluva lot more to him than a six-pack of beer.

I say that about John because I was in the same kind of boat. Until 1984, I had a serious problem with gambling, as close to an addiction as anyone outside Gamblers Anonymous ought to get. I could not *not* gamble. I lost as much as $10,000 in one six-week period of training camp. I lost $35,000 one year. I am a bad gambler. Terrible. The worst.

I asked my accountant one day, "Can I write off gambling losses?"

He said, "Yes, if you report gambling winnings."

"I never win," I said with perfect honesty.

Never. This is not a guy who wins $1,000 today and loses it tomorrow. I *never* won. Did I ever take lessons? No. To play blackjack, all you need is to be able to count to 21. And if you can't do that, the guy on the other side of the table will count for you.

All you need to do is push your money forward. If you don't have arms, you can push it up with your nose. Anything to gamble. That's the way it was for me for a long time. But I couldn't admit it was unhealthy. I hid my problem from everyone, including myself, by saying: "I don't have a gambling problem. I just like to play cards. So what if I lose money every single time? I keep coming back because I like it so much."

The gambling started at Notre Dame, where, as George Gipp had done 35 years earlier, I'd shoot pool for three or four hours every afternoon in the Student Union. Mostly 9-ball. We'd play for $25 to $100 a ball, and in a good year I might make $2,500 hustling under the Golden Dome.

Gambling was my way of being a big shot. When I went

to the Redskins in 1974, I wangled my way into card games. Every weekend in George Allen's Old Folks Home we had a card game. If you weren't playing football, you might as well play poker. On the bus to the airport, we'd play liar's poker. On the plane, it was real poker. On the bus from the airport to the hotel, more liar's poker. Morning, noon, and night. On land and in the air. Deal 'em, Joe.

Coach Allen finally got wind of the games and said: "I want no gambling. If there's anybody caught gambling, it's a game suspension."

So to make up the dead time in my gambling life, during the offseason I'd take an occasional trip to Las Vegas. I even went to Vegas on my honeymoon in 1970. And spent my entire wedding night at the table. By myself.

I couldn't stay away from the tables. In Vegas, my line of credit would be $5,000 at two or three casinos. There'd be checks for $500 here, for $1,000 there.

The ABC-TV Superstars competition in the Bahamas was always fun, and not because of the thrill of victory or agony of defeat. It was the thrill of the casino. With a guaranteed $2,000 in my pocket from the competition, I could walk into the casino already bankrolled.

Now we're talking big-time trouble, because if I had ever been lucky with that money and won, say, $25,000, I'd have lost $100,000 in the next hour.

I never, never, never won, for one simple reason: I was never satisfied with winning any amount of money. If I was $2,000 up, I wanted to be $5,000 up. I didn't just want to win, I wanted to break the bank. Give me Las Vegas. Move over, Howard Hughes. Nothing less. Throwing deep on every down. If I had thousand-dollar stacks in front of me, I'd bet the thousand. Forget the fact it took me three hours to win a thousand. I would double it in a minute. Just start throwing deep. Throw the bomb. Go deep, go long. I'll drop one on you. One out of 50 will land in the receiver's hands, right? Well, that's stupid football. It's more than stupid gambling, because when you lose three in a row gambling, there are no more bombs to throw. You're busted.

By the time Coach Gibbs came to the Redskins in 1981, the card games were going again full force. We'd have Russ Grimm, Mark May, Curtis Jordan, George Starke, Greg Williams, Tony Peters. We had a casino in the sky. On our plane trips in '85, we had cribbage games, backgammon, poker, and gin. All for money, of course. Richie Petitbon always came back to ask, "Howya doin', Joe?" The answer usually was, "Bad," and Richie would say, "Good, keep it up."

These games were important to me not because I made any money. Believe me, I wrote checks to everybody. On any list of people in this world with card sense, you won't find my name.

I raised poker bets for no reason whatsoever. Somebody would say, "You didn't even look at your cards."

"So what? I feel good about them."

I went into card games intending to quit as soon as $100 disappeared. Well, that took five minutes. Hell, there's the whole night ahead, it's training camp, I'll be bored to death if I quit. Out comes the ol' checkbook. Besides which, if Pigeon Joe didn't show up for a game, the guys sent a cab. Actually, they had so much of my money they could have sent a limo.

It was a way to pass the time in training camp when there was absolutely nothing to do. One night, somebody "pennied" us in. Seven of us had a game going in the lounge of Adams Hall at Dickinson College in Carlisle. If you lifted the lounge door just right, you could slip a penny in the lock and nobody could turn the knob. Russ Grimm had no conscience about it. He'd penny you in before breakfast at 7A.M. so you'd be late.

Anyway, it was one o'clock in the morning and we couldn't get out of the lounge, which is on the second floor. Being masters of football strategy, we used logic. It was a two-story fall to the ground; the tallest guy had the shortest fall. So we hung Clint Didier out the second-story window and told him to jump to the roof of the dorm porch below.

A two-story fall can kill a guy. But we almost had Clint convinced. He's about 6′5″, and you had these seven football players holding him out a window. We tried to be quiet, but we were laughing like kids trying to find a way out of this room without getting our star tight end killed. Finally we pulled Clint back in and banged on the door until we woke up a rookie. If you jostle the door from the outside, the penny falls down and you can get it open. We were free at last.

Joe Gibbs let our card games go through '82, '83, and '84, our best seasons. But he broke them up the next year by running two bed checks after curfew. This tells you something about how championship teams let things slide. Coaches start worrying about stuff other than football. The card games weren't a team problem, and since they let us do it in the good years and then clamped down as soon as we lost a few games, it upset everybody. We shouldn't have wasted any emotion or energy on such petty things, but we did, and maybe, added to a hundred other little things like that, you lose the hungry edge that wins a game you might otherwise lose.

You can't be uptight and win big. You gotta have fun. You gotta hang a guy out the window by his pants leg. Or trash a dorm. We trashed Adams Hall at the end of training camp in '82—and we went to our first Super Bowl five months later.

The dormitory went up in smoke, sort of, when we had a veteran–rookie war. We veterans put on our battle uniforms. Mine was a kimono I had bought in Hawaii. I tied a handkerchief around my forehead. Rambo in drag. Our linebacker, Richie Milot, strapped a fire extinguisher to his back. Monte Coleman, another linebacker, wore his football helmet and goggles. Neal Olkewicz rubbed dirt across his face. Our arsenal included water balloons, shaving cream, pillows, and fire hoses. This was a commando operation to celebrate the end of camp. We warmed up with a couple hours of beer at the Gingerbread Man, a tavern in Carlisle.

So Captain Bubbly is running around in his kimono and Milot looks like a freak with a flamethrower and guys are carrying buckets of water. Now we're creeping up the stairs to the fourth floor, where the rookies sleep. We're the cagey veterans, right? We're sneaking up the stairwell when we hear, "Yaaaaaah!"

There's a ten-gallon garbage can full of water and some rookie has tipped it over on us. There's a waterfall coming down the stairwell. Now we're slipping and sliding up the steps and we break through the fourth-floor door. We don't see anybody. They're all hiding in their rooms. They've got furniture and mattresses stacked against the doors.

We go banging on the doors and breaking them down. Our Commando Harrys are shooting hoses under doors. We're setting off the fire extinguishers into the rooms. Rookies come out gagging and coughing. We spray them with shaving cream and bomb them with water balloons.

We throw firecrackers into the johns, we light smoke bombs in the corridors. There's this fog, a mist, a cloud hanging everywhere—Saigon after a bombing. Beds are leaning against the walls. Mattresses are thrown everywhere. The floors are a total mess.

We, the veterans, declare total victory. And I go to bed, a happy camper. What do I hear an hour later? Knock, knock on my door.

"Yeah?" I say.

Our line coach, LaVern Torgerson, says, "Get up!"

"Huh?"

Torgy says, "Get out here and clean up this mess."

"But Torgy . . ."

"Don't give me any of that shit, Theismann. Get a mop and clean it up!"

So, in total victory, and from one to three A.M., Captain Bubbly mopped the floors. Me, alone, by myself. I gave away no secrets about the operation. The coaches tortured me with razor-thin strips of steel inserted under my fingernails. They threatened to take away my hair lightener. Still I refused to reveal the names of my commando troops. I print their names now at this late date only to honor them and to ask, "Which one of you bums took my kimono?"

I was talking about gambling. I've quit it now, and not out of any moral or Biblical sense that it's wrong. I just got tired of giving money away. I'd have been better off taking 35,000 dollar bills, putting them in a pile, and having a wienie roast.

I've lost TV sets. I owed a wide receiver $500 and paid him off with a backgammon board. Need a VCR? Just get ol' Joe in a card game and chances are you can win one. The gambling was just one more way to create artificial excitement, to get attention. Cathy Lee helped me out of that rathole and in the process helped me get control of the gambling.

She never said, "Don't gamble." She'd go with me to the casino and sit there and say: "Go ahead, bet it all. Go ahead, bet. Bet it all."

We'd have been there five minutes, so I'd say no, I want to stay. Cathy Lee would have none of my excuses. "Go ahead, bet it all," she'd say. "You're going to lose it all, anyway. You might as well lose it quickly so we can move on to something more fun." When she said that, something snapped and I have had control ever since.

I never bet on a football or baseball or basketball game. This shows you the warped mind of the gambler. I'd go to a casino and bet on some stupid cards, but I would never bet on sporting events, which I presumably know something about. That's because the sport is sacred to me, and I could not violate it. Not everyone shares my beliefs. One of Pete Rozelle's first bold moves as commissioner of the NFL was to suspend Paul Hornung and Alex Karras for a season when they were found to have bet on their own teams to win. That was more than 20 years ago and no one has been suspended since. But don't believe that the lack of suspensions means that players no longer make bets on football; they're just not getting caught. I know a player who bet $10,000 on his own team to win the Super Bowl. He played well and his team won. I assume there must be players on every team who bet on games. But it's hard to imagine any guys who'd have the nerve to bet *against* their own teams.

This kind of talk always leads to the question, "Could you fix a pro football game?" I don't think so. A lot of people say it can be done. They say you can fix any game that exists. Maybe I'm naive.

No gambler has ever approached anyone I know to fix a game. It just seems impossible. Only four or five people seem to be in the position to fix a game. The quarterback is the first. A kicker is next. Then a wide receiver, a defensive back, and a running back. These people handle the ball. They put points on the board—and could keep points from going up.

But how could there be a fix without making it so obvious? Football is different from basketball, where if you just miss a layup you can control who wins all the bets. But in football it might take a touchdown, and that's not so easy to arrange. Then you've got trouble—either with the police or the bad guys betting the other way. And it's not a one-time deal. If you get bought once, they're not going to be satisfied with just getting you one time. Gamblers can't make enough money in a one-time hit. They want a big return on their investment, and if they don't get it, who knows what they'll do?

We're talking a risky world here. Too risky for a quarterback who gets into enough trouble just playing poker with the guys.

14
The Ultimate
Game ... Again

T he Redskins had become a truly great team, a group of guys who would absolutely put their rear ends on the line for their teammates. That was what Joe Gibbs wanted, and that's what he got. He also preached patience and demanded intelligence, and he got those, too. Mostly, Gibbs and his coaches wanted us to be a tough, physical, take-no-prisoners team. They wanted guys who beat the hell out of people. They wanted guys who could win the "Leather Balls Award."

Every week at a team meeting, we'd award the Leather Balls to a guy who went out there and completely showed no respect for his own body. It was two ball bearings in a leather sack. If you won it, you also got your own parking place for the week at Redskin Park. Special-teams crazies like Otis Wonsley and Pete Cronan won it. Linebackers who flew downfield on the suicide squads won it. John Riggins, Joe Jacoby, Russ Grimm—the down and dirty Hogs—they won it. Guys who liked to walk around the locker room with blood dripping down the bridge of their noses.

The more physical we played, the better we were. And the more we ran the ball, the more physical we became. We were always stronger than the other team at the end of the game because we practiced harder. We were the only team in the NFL that played four games a week. We hit on Wednesday, Thursday, Friday—we hit hard—and on Sunday we finally got to hit the other guys. So we'd be just about getting cranked up in the fourth quarter, when John was up to 25 carries. By then, Grimm's nose was bleeding a river and Jacoby was clearing people out like King Kong running through the forest.

Joe Gibbs had developed this power game for several reasons. We had a bunch of little-bitty receivers, everybody 5'9" and not very fast. Our tight end Rick Walker couldn't catch anything on the left side of the field because his musculature wouldn't allow him to turn his head to the left far enough to see the ball coming. Meanwhile, we had Riggo raring to run (he would say in the huddle, "Guess it's time we got started," and so we did). We also had offensive-line monsters named Grimm, Jacoby, Mark May, Jeff Bostic, and Donnie Warren.

Russ Grimm is a 290-pound guard who sometimes arranged himself in the shower so the water wouldn't wash away the blood caked on his face. Russ is the ultimate offensive lineman. Strong, big, quick, with a dangerous sense of humor, especially in an airplane. Russ loves to fly. A lot of guys don't. Russ would sit there in the plane, stare out the window, and scream: "The wheels are falling off! Oh my God! Look at that engine—it's on fire! Just like in my dream—we were at 30,000 feet and the plane started to shake, just like this, and then . . . oh, my God!" You could see Dexter Manley's knuckles turn white.

The only time I ever heard Russ Grimm bitch about anything, it was Mark May's doing. Mark was at right tackle down in Dallas across the line from John Dutton, the least feared of the Cowboys defensive line, which also included Ed Jones, Harvey Martin, and Randy White. On certain plays, Mark would cut-block White, and maybe grace him with a few choice words. If he couldn't reach White, he'd scream about White's family heritage.

And since those folks couldn't get at Mark, they'd just beat the daylights out of Grimm while May was dancing late-da with Dutton. Finally, in the third quarter, Russ blew up. "Dammit, May Day, shut up! Randy's gonna kill me!"

Good fortune helps invention, too, as Joe Gibbs learned the first time he ever saw Joe Jacoby, who is 6'7" and 325 pounds. Jacoby came to camp as a free agent out of Louisville, drafted by nobody, and line coach Joe Bugel took him to meet Gibbs, who glanced up and said, "Sorry, we've got enough defensive linemen, we really don't need another one."

Bugel quickly explained that Joe was an offensive tackle, only in the extra-large size.

Joe Gibbs just had never seen an offensive lineman so big. Within three seasons, Joe Jacoby was All-Pro.

As good as we were in '82, we were better in '83. We lived in Dreamland. Everything worked for us. We scored 541 points, which is 34 a game, almost five touchdowns every Sunday. Nobody had ever done that. John Riggins ran for 1,347 yards and an NFL record 24 touchdowns. I was named the league's MVP after having my best year (29 touchdown passes, almost 4,000 yards).

We had set the NFL scoring record against the most sophisticated defenses ever used, the defenses of the '80s. We were a precision machine equal to the best Green Bay teams, the best Dolphins, the best Steelers. I wear a Super Bowl ring today because the Redskins of '82 had all the elements that identify championship teams. You must have four or five guys clearly more physically gifted than any four or five on any other team. You need at least four Pro Bowl people; with six, you'll be in the Super Bowl unless something strange happens. We had five men in the '83 Pro Bowl and seven in the '84 game. (And that's without John Riggins making it. His omission was a crime. No running back ever carried a team the way John carried us). What a feeling of confidence. Anytime I stepped onto a field in those seasons, I knew we couldn't be beaten. If we didn't beat you with passing, we'd do it by running over you. Or we'd run a punt back or take away a fumble. Whatever it took, there was the attitude we would do it.

Winning, like losing, is contagious. You go into a game knowing you're going to win at some point. Don't ask me how you can *know* that. You just do. It's confidence in yourself and your teammates that someone will do what's necessary when it's necessary.

Who, for that matter, can explain what happened in 1979 to our center, Ted Fritsch? I saw his career disintegrate in one day. For three seasons, he had been the confident Mr. Steady, a co-captain of our special teams, one of the best long snappers in the league. But down at Tampa for a pre-season game in '79, Ted suddenly started air-mailing the ball. It went over the kicker's head, it went sideways, it went haywire.

No one knew what was wrong. Ted just couldn't snap the ball anymore. His father had died about that time, so maybe it was the trauma of the death, but Ted never made any excuses. He couldn't straighten it out. And within three days he was released because he just couldn't snap it accurately anymore. His confidence was shot. It was the damnedest thing I've ever seen in football. And none of us is immune to such sudden failure. Everyone in the NFL lives on the edge.

In 1983 we lived on top. We won 14 regular-season games and lost two, both by one point. Riggo was unstoppable. Mark Moseley's kicking was sensational, as always. Returning punts, Mike Nelms was phenomenal. You'd see him stopped dead in his tracks by defenders, and somehow, a second later, he'd be running down the sidelines with one guy chasing him.

This is how confident we had become. The week before a game, I would ask Richie Petitbon, our defensive coordinator, "How many points you need?" He might say, "We can keep 'em in the 10–14 range. You get 21, we'll win." Or maybe: "They're a tough ball club. Gimme everything you got. And if you find a little more, throw that in there, too, 'cause we may need it."

We enjoyed the season as much as the fans did. At our first team meeting after a game, we would look at film highlights of the best plays, like a Nelms return, a Moseley kick (he'd get booed because everyone gave him a hard time about kickers not being real football players), or a defensive effort by Dave Butz or Dexter Manley.

One of our favorite movies of '83 showed Joe Jacoby against the Los Angeles Rams. Jake blocked the defensive end. Then he blocked a linebacker. Then a cornerback. All on the same play, and I shouldn't say he *blocked* anybody. It was like a building demolition. Bodies were flying upside down and everwhere.

Watching the highlight package gives you a sense of camaraderie. It feeds your ego. Hey, it's fun, and there is a lot to be said for a football team having fun. There's too much pain to take if there's no reward for taking it. In George Allen's time, we were like six-year-olds at a birthday party on those Thursdays when Duke Zeibert brought us ice cream and cake after we won on Sunday.

You remember those little fun things, like finally being able to shut up my New Jersey jeering section at Giants Stadium. I almost never played very well there. The field has a high crown to it and the receivers seem to drop off the edge of the world when they run an out. The more I thought about how high the crown was, the higher it got, until you'd have thought I was pitching from off a mountaintop. It was not a place for quarterbacks with rabbit ears, either, and I definitely heard every word from my jeering section right behind the visitors bench. Of course, I never let them know it, until now.

"Hey, Joey Th*ee*sman," they'd yell, "you're no good, you're a bum." Right away you knew these people were from the area because they knew about my so-called name change. They'd come up from South Amboy and New

Brunswick to harass the old neighborhood boy. "I hope they tear your head off, Theesman."

They had a great time, especially when I'd go through one of my ritual superstitions after coming off the field. Whether I was thirsty or not, I'd pick up a cup of juice, take a sip, spit it out, and throw the cup away. Every time. And these people knew it. About 10 of them would chant: "Yeah, that's right, take the cup. Take a drink. Spit it out. Throw it in the trash. Yeah. You finally hit what you were aimin' at."

In '82 and '83, we won both our games in Giants Stadium. That made my drinking routine more enjoyable.

Our quarterback coach, Dan Henning, once said he forgets every victory and remembers every loss. He said that at Atlanta, where he was the head coach four seasons after leaving the Redskins. You work to win, you go out expecting to win, you win and you say, "Swell," and you get ready for the next game. But if you lose, it is unexpected and it hurts.

Of all our 1983 games, the Green Bay defeat stands out in my mind. On a Monday night, we lost, 48-47. Every time they scored, we'd come back and score. We had the ball last on our own 20 with about 30 seconds to play. I love these moments. We moved about 55 yards in five plays and got Mark Moseley a chance for a chip-shot field goal to win.

Only, he missed it and we lost. You can't get mad at Mark after all the games he's won. But I did. I was totally frustrated, to come that far and lose.

We beat people in '83 by scores such as 38-14 and 38-17, 45-7 and 42-20, 31-10 and 51-7. By the time we made it to the Super Bowl for a second straight season, we had won 16 of 18 games by an average score of 34-20. Our opponents in the Super Bowl were the Los Angeles Raiders, a team we'd beaten at RFK early in the season, 37-35.

So how come we lost to the Raiders, 38-9, in the most embarrassing game ever for a Joe Gibbs team?

No denying we were on a roll. We had won 31 of our last

34 games. The day of the Super Bowl, a *Washington Post* columnist listed 13 reasons why we could not possibly lose. Trouble is, we believed it. As exciting as the first Super Bowl had been, the second somehow left us flat. We came in stale, and possibly overprepared.

By Wednesday of that week, we had our game plan and we knew *everything* about the Raiders. I didn't like that feeling. I like a feeling of anticipation, mystery, not quite being sure what's going to happen. I don't necessarily want to know *everything*. I want to react to what the other team does.

Unlike the previous Super Bowl, when Joe Gibbs's eyes twinkled as he unfolded his "Explode Package" for our offense, we received nothing flashy-new for the Raiders. It was business as usual, which meant, of course, that yours truly spent nearly every working hour being Mr. Interview.

Morning TV shows, afternoon radio shows, late-night call-in shows, scheduled press conferences, impromptu press conferences. Our fans are wonderful and they were in Tampa full force—all of them, it seemed, in our hotel lobby. To get to the elevator, you needed a tank. For the first time ever, I got sick of talking. I felt like I'd played two Super Bowls that week, one on the field and one with my mouth.

On the bus going to our Friday workout, John Riggins said to me: "Our hotel is a zoo. If we go to another Super Bowl, I'm going to rent an apartment away from the hotel." I couldn't have agreed more.

Right. Next time.

Twenty-seven games later, Lawrence Taylor fell on my right leg. By then, the Redskins had traded to get George Rogers, a big running back. Riggo's days, like mine, were numbered. There would never be a "next time" for us. Sadly, our last Super Bowl was a miserable experience, and I should have known it was coming because all week I kept finding things to gripe about.

One day it was "too warm," the next day would be "too cold". And then there were my shoes. This is how far from

football my mind was. I had asked Pro-Keds to make me
some new shoes especially for the Super Bowl. They were
size 11, my size, but they were a bit too big because of the
soft leather they were made from. Instead of getting a pair
the right size, I just kept worrying about how these didn't fit
right.

What didn't fit right in the more important sense was our
team's attitude. We were the mighty Redskins. We had our
chins stuck out, and the Raiders decked us with a right
cross.

We couldn't run on them because their nose tackle,
Reggie Kinlaw, played the defensive game of his life. Every
time I looked up, safety Mike Davis seemed to be in my
face. Our defense couldn't stop Marcus Allen. And I
couldn't complete the important passes. The ball just kept
floating out there. I was 16 for 35 and was sacked six times.

My most memorable pass made Jack Squirek famous.
With ten seconds left in the first half, I threw a little screen
pass that Squirek intercepted and ran in for a touchdown
and a 21-3 lead that about killed us. Squirek was a reserve
linebacker. But you know what? I bet he didn't spend the
week bitching about the weather or how his shoes fit.

Afterward, Joe Gibbs was stunned and disappointed. I
don't remember what he said to us in the locker room,
partly because I only half-listen to anything in those
situations and partly because I knew every reporter in
America would be coming after me to hear about that
screen pass.

Why would you throw a screen pass from your own 10-
yard line with ten seconds left in the half? Well, we'd hit a
big play off that screen pass earlier in the season when we
beat the Raiders. So precedent was on our side. But the
Raiders wouldn't be easily fooled with the same play.

Anyway, unless we went 90 yards for a touchdown, even
a big play would get us nothing. Time would run out
before we could kick a field goal. We had called a timeout
to talk about what we wanted to do. When Joe said he
wanted to run the screen pass, I was surprised.

"You sure?" I said to him on the sidelines. He said yes, and I jogged back to the huddle, all the way thinking: "This is not going to work. Should I change the play? This is just not going to work."

We had reached the Super Bowl twice by following Joe's orders, and I had become a decent quarterback by giving up the improvisations of my youth. So I threw the damned thing, and it landed right in Squirek's hands.

When the reporters came to me afterward, they wanted an explanation of why we would run such a high-risk play in that situation. I said: "It's not the play that's called, it's the way it's executed. I executed it poorly."

That wasn't a total lie. I should have seen Squirek. It wasn't the whole truth, either. Not being able to run against the Raiders in the first half had thrown Joe Gibbs out of his normal play-calling rhythm. Had we moved the ball on the ground, he would never have called a screen pass so deep in our own territory. He was looking for a play to get us going.

It was ludicrous to call that play.

The truth is, it was lousy execution by Joe Theismann of a lousy call by Joe Gibbs.

15
A Gift from Heaven

In 1984, after our Super Bowl loss, I finally OD'd on talk. I decided to talk to the press only after games, and then only about games. *Sports Illustrated*'s editors thought that was so incredible they put me on the cover of the September 3 issue—and then they had an artist superimpose tape over my mouth. But they didn't bother to explain that they had superimposed the tape, so it appeared that I had posed for a gag photo. I didn't. The cover headline read, " 'How the Skins gonna do this year, Joe?' 'Mmph.' "

I just wanted to play football. Also, about that time, I had started dating Cathy Lee Crosby, and I knew that the questions about my personal life would be included in every interview. My life had been an open book until then, and I wanted to change that.

The first time I actually met Cathy Lee Crosby was in 1980 at a Special Olympics event in Stowe, Vermont. I introduced myself, we shook hands and said hello. That was that.

We met again in May of 1983 when Cathy Lee was a presenter at the Victor Awards in Las Vegas. Again, the encounter was brief. I reintroduced myself (she had forgotten our earlier meeting—great for the ego) and that was about it.

Later that night we had a chance to talk. She asked, among other things, if I was married. I told her I was, and she said, "That's wonderful." A short time later she left, and once again, that was that.

I can't say exactly what it was that I felt after meeting Cathy Lee that second time, but I do remember thinking: "Not only is she beautiful but she seems like a very special person."

In March of 1984, after my separation, my thoughts kept wandering to Cathy Lee. I decided to take a chance and call her. "Would you be interested in going to dinner?"

She said, "No."

Regrouping my forces, I called again in April. "I'm going to be on the coast next week. Would you like to have dinner some night?"

Again she said, "No," but added, "Look, you're a great guy and all, but I'm just not interested."

Later in April, I called again. "Dinner?" "No."

Let me say this: Joe Theismann has never been a Don Juan. I dated one girl in high school and had only two dates my first two years at Notre Dame. But this was ridiculous.

I decided to gather all my courage for one last assault, and I called again at the beginning of June. "I'm going to be on the coast this week [using a familiar line], how about dinner?"

And before she could say no, I immediately began to plead my case. If this was going to be my last shot, I was going to give it my all.

"Look, what harm could come of it? It's just dinner, and you can even meet me at the restaurant if that makes you feel better. You have to eat anyway, and besides, I'm not taking no for an answer." Perhaps influenced by the hand of fate, but most definitely influenced by one highly convincing argument by yours truly, she relented.

So on June 5, 1984, we finally sat down to dinner, and my life has never been the same since.

The evening was wonderful. We talked about everything, almost as if we had known each other forever. The next morning I called and asked her to go to the beach. When I was growing up in New Jersey, for me the beach was a place of wonderful memories, and suddenly, for the first time in my life, I wanted to share that feeling with someone. Not with just anyone and not just anywhere, but with Cathy Lee at the beach.

I felt like a kid again, like somehow my life was starting over. We walked and talked and wrestled and ran and played, and I knew that I was in love, for the first time in my life. Deeply, passionately, unselfishly in love.

As we sat and watched the sunset, I turned to her and said simply, "I'm going to spend the rest of my life with you." I wasn't bragging or feeding her a line. I was speaking from the heart. She didn't say a word. She just looked at me and I knew she knew.

As we became more involved, I felt like I was living a dream. Except that things were moving at 45 rpms instead of my typical 33 ⅓. Now, people have on occasion accused me of moving at a fast pace; with Cathy Lee, we're talking whirlwind. I was struggling just to keep up with her. She is not a person who merely gets an idea—oh, she gets ideas, all right, lots of them—but she acts on *all* of them, too—immediately.

I thought I was in good shape; well, forget it. I soon found out what being in shape really meant. Up at six, work out at seven, tennis at nine, to the office by eleven, lunch (forget it), dance class at three, racquetball at five, dinner (I begged), a movie at eight, backgammon at ten, and, thank God, asleep by midnight. And that's just a normal day (except, of course, when she's filming). She just loves life, and that love is contagious.

We soon found out how much we had in common. We

both loved to travel, we loved sports and competition, we loved romance and adventure and sharing on an intimate level. I was also beginning to realize that this was the first time I had ever been willing to share my life totally with anyone. I felt comfortable enough with Cathy Lee to say whatever I needed to say, even my deepest secrets, because I knew she understood. Equally as important, she felt safe enough to share her feelings with me, and I wanted to listen.

I had always felt that I didn't need anyone, that I could handle any situation myself. Asking for help somehow made me feel inferior. But when I opened up to Cathy Lee, I found a part of myself that I never knew existed, a part I really liked. It opened my eyes to a whole new set of priorities. One very big step for Joe Theismann.

She also helped me learn to look at life and to laugh, even at myself. She has that special ability to take the most serious moments and find humor. For example, four days after I broke my leg, I was lying in traction waiting for my gin partner and teammate Mark May to come visit for the first time. He hates hospitals, but we were such close friends that he was coming anyway. Cathy Lee turned to me and I saw that twinkle in her eye.

"What are you up to now?" I asked, not really wanting to hear the answer.

She just smiled as she began to pour ketchup on my forehead and cast. "Close your eyes and start to moan when he walks in."

Already committed to this because I'm covered with ketchup, I did just that. When Mark walked in, he stopped and stared, and, visibly shaken, turned to Cathy Lee and asked if I was all right.

Just about that time I started to laugh. He had expected me to be full of needles and all covered with blood, and the break to be visible. So the joke broke the tension and we all had a good laugh.

But that was nothing compared to the time we were in Dallas during the 1984 season, playing the Cowboys for a chance to clinch the division title for the third consecutive year. I kept calling Cathy Lee throughout the week and telling her how important the game was—it was going to be another classic Redskin–Cowboy slugfest, and I felt a lot of pressure to play my absolute best.

The night before the game I walked into my hotel room, and there, standing before me, was Danny White. Well, not *quite* Danny White. It was a mannequin, dressed in full Cowboy uniform, number 11, complete with helmet, shoulder pads, and shoes. Not to mention arrows sticking through him, the jersey torn, and red dye and bruises all over his body. I just kept shaking my head in disbelief. The next day, as Danny and I stood face to face on the field, I could hardly keep a straight face. But the important thing was that I played pressure-free and we were lucky enough to win.

Having finally learned the value of humor in difficult situations, I took advantage of the opportunity to play a joke of my own. Cathy Lee was in the midst of filming a movie and was concerned about how things were going. She had reached a creative impasse and didn't know what to do. So I thought she could use a little something to cheer her up.

The next day I had a ten-foot tree delivered to her trailer on the lot. They couldn't actually get the tree into the trailer, so they left it right in front of her door. Meanwhile, she was inside dressing and didn't have the slightest knowledge of the delivery. So when they called her to the set, she couldn't get out the door. And of course, this became the source of incessant teasing from cast and crew. Joe, 7; Tension, 0.

We also share a love for adventure. Of course, my idea of adventure and her idea of adventure do not remotely resemble each other. I like to fly, she likes to fly trapeze; I like to high dive, she likes to sky dive; I like to ride horses in the country, she likes to ride horses in *another* country.

Which reminds me of my first big adventure á la Cathy Lee. She was working in Ecuador when she called to tell me she wouldn't be home for at least a couple of weeks. Well, I didn't want to wait that long to see her, and besides, what's a little trip to South America? So I told her I'd be there the next day.

Pretty big statement from a guy whose only adventure outside North America was a four-day trip to England. She tried to dissuade me, but my mind was set.

The next day, as I walked down the steps of the plane, I was greeted by uniformed guards with rifles and pistols. It looked like something out of "Mission: Impossible." Hmmm, maybe this wasn't such a good idea after all. I was led to customs, and I suddenly realized I couldn't understand a word anyone was saying.

Then, out of nowhere, there was this surge from the crowd, and everyone was yelling and screaming, *"Lo increible! Lo increible!"* I had no idea what was going on, and I began to panic. Only two things in my life have ever truly frightened me: the 1982 mob scene in RFK when we beat the Cowboys for the conference championship, and the rush of that screaming crowd in Ecuador.

The next thing I knew, someone grabbed my arm and yelled, "Come this way, we have a car waiting!" It was Cathy Lee. Fighting our way through the melee, I suddenly realized that all the fuss was over her. The people had seen a glimpse of their favorite TV star—"That's Incredible" was the top-rated show in the country at the time. As it turned out, there were crowds like that wherever we went, and I eventually got used to playing bodyguard for Cathy Lee.

Then there was Japan, and Antigua, and St. Martin. Spin the globe and point your fingers, the chances were good that Cathy Lee had plane reservations to go there. So now I keep a suitcase packed and my mind open, and I wait to see which way the winds will blow us next.

I did, however, draw the line at raising a deer in the house. Cathy Lee has this friend who is a real animal lover—you know: ten dogs, six cats, horses, the works—and she was telling us how she had raised a deer. Well, I could see Cathy Lee's wheels start turning. I sat back, praying silently that there was no way she could possibly ask me to raise a deer at our farm in Leesburg, Virginia. Of course, she thought it was a great idea, that it would give our dog, C.J., someone to play with, and that if Michael Jackson could raise a pet llama, we could have a deer.

Now, we've had our farm for about two years, and in that time we've raised horses, cattle, snakes, rabbits, and even a rooster, many of which have spent time inside the house. But what in the world was I going to do with a deer? I'm going to come home and find a deer curled up on the couch next to the dog? I had enough trouble paper-training the rabbit; I wasn't going to start with a deer. Finally, after four months of explaining why our house wasn't big enough for both me and a deer, Cathy Lee relented. I just hope she isn't thinking about a llama.

I've always been a romantic at heart, but for some reason I never wanted to express it. Oh, I would buy Christmas presents and offer those typically expected expressions of affection, but that was the extent of it. Now, I don't feel I need a special occasion to show my love. Flowers, phone calls, poems, cards, anything that tells Cathy Lee how much she means to me. And it didn't take long to discover that I wasn't the only romantic in the relationship. She kept the florist busy, too.

I remember when she first started sending me roses; in particular, roses sent to Redskin Park. This gave my teammates a whole new source of entertainment. They'd switch cards, make up their own messages, and wait for my reaction.

Once they changed the card to read: "You have the greatest buns. Love, Bruce." I'm trying to hide the card, pretend that nothing is wrong, and Rick Walker, one of our tight ends, asks me (loudly), "What's the card say, Joe?"

"Ahh, nothing, Rick," I stammered.

"C'mon, Joe, read us the card," he persisted.

He kept hounding me until finally he asked if it was from Bruce. Then he grinned, handed me the original card, and walked away like the cat triumphant.

The coaches, on the other hand, didn't tease me at all. In fact, they eagerly awaited the arrival of Cathy Lee's flowers. I couldn't figure it out. One day the flowers didn't come, and coach Warren Simmons, extremely concerned, asked where they were. I explained that they had been sent to my restaurant instead. Oh, he responded, that was a shame, because he needed a couple to take home to his wife. Seems he and the other coaches had been using my roses for their own romantic gestures. And now I understand why they were so sorry to see me retire.

You might think that this sounds too good to be true, that no one has a relationship like ours. Well, all I can say is that I'm talking straight from my heart, and it's true, every word of it. Cathy Lee has been in my corner 100 percent, and not always with things I wanted to hear. She has taught me to appreciate the simple things in life. She has helped me to understand how important respect is in a relationship, particularly self-respect. She has shared her gentleness, warmth, and caring with someone who had to learn how to share. She has taught me the true meaning of love and family.

It doesn't mean we don't have disagreements or misunderstandings, because we do. It simply means that we have a bottom line that is very special, and a bond of love and commitment that we both want to last forever. I thank God every day for the privilege of being able to share my life and love with her. .

16
Thank You,
Mr. Cooke

Jack Kent Cooke is a multimillionaire who made his money the old-fashioned way: he earned it. Around 1932, with nothing but energy, enthusiasm, a salesman's charm, and ingenuity, he drove all over Canada selling what he called "perfectly dreadful encyclopedias." Before he was 30, he was the millionaire partner of Lord Roy Thomson in radio stations and newspapers. A writer once approached Mr. Cooke and said, "I'd like to include you in a book I'm doing on the five greatest salesmen in the world."

Mr. Cooke said, "Sir, I am not one of *five* anything."

A man of Mr. Cooke's wealth is not in football for the money, but for the fun. More than all the real estate and business deals, owning the Redskins is the greatest joy Mr. Cooke has outside his family.

He has been a winner in sports for almost 35 years. He began in baseball in Toronto, where he owned the Maple Leafs of the International League. He once passed up a chance to buy the Detroit Tigers. In the early '60s Branch

Rickey wanted to start a third major league, the Continental League, and he asked Mr. Cooke to be a partner. But before the Continental League could take off, the National League expanded by creating the Houston Astros and New York Mets. The expansion killed off Mr. Rickey's idea.

Mr. Cooke moved from Canada to Los Angeles, where he bought the Lakers and created the Los Angeles Kings hockey team. In 1972, with hockey attendance down, a reporter said the decrease was strange because 800,000 Canadians lived in Los Angeles. "I've just discovered why they left Canada," Mr. Cooke said. "They hate hockey."

Almost on a dare by the city of Los Angeles, which wouldn't give him a fair lease on the Sports Arena, Mr. Cooke built his own arena. He built it on a grand scale. He called it "The Fabulous Forum." And soon enough, with that desire to win that makes him special, Mr. Cooke had one of the greatest basketball teams ever, the Lakers, with Jerry West, Elgin Baylor, and Wilt Chamberlain.

Mr. Cooke noticed everything. When Jerry West coached the Lakers, Mr. Cooke saw a new player on the court, Johnny Neumann, brought in from the defunct American Basketball Association. This is the story Jerry tells:

"This Neumann fellow," Mr. Cooke said to Jerry, "is he overweight?"

"About eight pounds," Jerry said.

"Here's what I want you to do, Jerry. Go to the meat market and buy an eight-pound roast and lash it to Mr. Neumann's waist. Then he will know how heavy those eight extra pounds are."

The first sign that Mr. Cooke will be at a Redskin practice is the appearance on the sideline of three chairs: one for Mr. Cooke, one for his son John Kent Cooke (now the executive vice president of the Redskins), and one for a guest.

The second sign is that Joe Gibbs gets nervous. He knows the big eye is watching. Everything has to be precise. The word for Joe on those days is "intense." Really intense.

He wants the show to be a good one because the boss is there.

Mr. Cooke often has someone with him, such as writer Stephen King, and he'll call over players to introduce them. You'd be all embarrassed because the guys would give you grief, like, "Oh, OK, Joe, you're going over to see Dad now."

Well, as soon as I got my last contract—worth $4.5 million for four years—I said to the guys, "Yep, go ahead, call him Dad, that's fine with me." Mr. Cooke was as fair and generous with me as any man could expect, and I have nothing but respect and admiration for him. Oh, maybe a little twinge of gut fear once in a while, but that's only a leftover from those days when I thought he was God.

The first eight years of my Redskin career, he was only an imperious voice coming through the phone. In 1978 George Allen called me into his office and said, "I've got somebody on the phone who wants to talk to you." It was Mr. Cooke calling from his home in Las Vegas, and by the tone of our conversation it seemed pretty clear he liked the way I played. Of course, George still wanted Billy Kilmer in there. Too bad Mr. Cooke wasn't the coach as well as the owner.

We met for the first time at a team banquet in 1979, and talked about the season coming up. Mr. Cooke was animated, as always, and said he expected big things from us. Only he said it this way: "Ah, but a man's reach should exceed his grasp/Or what's a heaven for?" He smiled at me. "Browning," Mr. Cooke said.

By certain design, Mr. Cooke was an intimidating force. I learned this the first time I negotiated a contract directly with him instead of Edward Bennett Williams, his long-time minority partner. It was 1982. My agent, Ed Keating, and I were in Mr. Cooke's office at Kent Farm, near Middleburg, Virginia. We had agreed on the contract, but Ed and I needed to talk about a detail, so we left the office for a minute. As I had walked through the house earlier, I noticed Mr. Cooke's paintings. Millions of dollars worth of paintings, probably. There I was wanting a contract for $1 million over four years. Hell, any one of the paintings on his wall was worth more than my services.

When Ed and I came back to his office, Mr. Cooke said, "You know, Joe, I'm not going to give you what we talked about."

WHAT? My mind started racing. *Why, you son of a . . .* Luckily, I didn't say a thing. I was scared into silence. Totally intimidated. I was in no position to argue with a tycoon. I was a Polaroid snapshot in a roomful of Renoirs.

There was a silence in the office until Mr. Cooke said, "No, I'm going to give you *more.*"

He did, too, $50,000 on the spot. I was overwhelmed. I was ecstatic.

I was also stupid, because the first thing I did was go on television and try to quote Mr. Cooke so I could convey some of the unique flavor of our negotiation. The contract was a real breakthrough after all the years behind Kilmer, and I said as much on the tube.

Shortly after the six o'clock news, the phone rang in my restaurant. It was God calling from Middleburg. Mr. Cooke said in his very strong voice, "First of all, Joseph, I don't talk like that."

Uh-oh.

Then he said, "I've got half a mind to tear up this contract."

Remembering that I had a signed contract did nothing to make me feel better. The $50,000 extra wasn't enough to buy the aspirin this headache would need.

Even later, after two Super Bowls, I was still worried that Mr. Cooke, at the slightest offense, would cut me. Release me. Just fire me and tell the world: "He never heard of Browning and he misquoted me. He can't play in the NFL that way."

Maybe it's silly to think an owner would cut the quarterback who took his team to the Super Bowl, but that's the way my mind worked. I lived in fear of Jack Kent Cooke. And that fear was still active when we discussed my next contract. At the time, John Elway and Dan Fouts each made $1 million a year; Joe Theismann made $300,000 and ranked 20th among quarterback salaries.

So, as usual, I contracted my famous hoof-in-mouth disease and made statements in the newspapers and on TV about wanting a new contract. Soon enough the telephone rang. Mr. Cooke said, "I'd like to see you."

It's a 45-minute drive from Washington to Mr. Cooke's house in the Virginia countryside. Rolling pastures. Mountains in the distance. It's a beautiful drive—unless you've said something foolish (again) about the man who owns your contract.

Regarding an unfair contract, a gentleman and decent person might have said, "Mr. Cooke, would you please examine my compensation package as it relates to those of other successful quarterbacks in the National Football League and see if any adjustment can be made?"

But I popped off in the newspapers and then waited for something to happen. It came in the form of that phone call. So I made the lonnnggg drive to Mr. Cooke's farm. And when I got there, he laced into me. When he finished, if there had been an ant on the floor, I'd have been looking up at that ant. But at least he never said, "I'm going to punish you by letting you play out this current contract and never giving you what you think you're worth."

After that the contract negotiations were done in private, not in the newspaper. It was one of the strangest "negotiations" ever.

We talked for two years. We had basically agreed to terms before the 1985 season in a session at his office. I went there dead-set determined to get my figure. Elway and Fouts hadn't won a championship; I had been in two Super Bowls. As Mr. Cooke took out some papers, I had a figure in mind. I was prepared. I had done my homework. Mr. Cooke said, "Take a look at this, Joe."

It was a breakdown of what my contract would be.

It was, be still my heart, for more money than I had in mind.

Mr. Cooke also said I should insure the contract. He wrote down the approximate premium cost, about $35,000, and the names of some agents and companies.

Thirty-five-thousand might not seem like much out of $4.5 million. But a lot of my salary was deferred to later years. So my current annual cash was about $400,000. Half went to Uncle Sam. Of the $200,000 left, my expenses ate into that. Suddenly, that $35,000 seemed like big money.

"I really need that money," I said to Mr. Cooke. "And besides, I'm not going to get hurt. I don't need any insurance. I'm going to play out this contract."

Mr. Cooke then explained that I was insuring the $4.5 million deal for less than one percent of the total. He also said: "Joe, do not deduct the premium from your income taxes. If you deduct it, you must pay income taxes on any benefit. If you don't deduct it, the entire benefit is yours."

Without Mr. Cooke's advice, I would not have taken out the insurance or if I had, I certainly would have deducted the premium cost. The second day I was in the hospital with my broken leg, Mr. Cooke came by. He asked, "Joe, did you insure the contract?"

"Yes, sir."

"The premium, Joe, did you deduct it on your tax return?"

"No, sir."

"Attaboy," Mr. Cooke said.

Though we'd agreed on most aspects of the deal, we didn't actually sign the contract until February of 1986— three months *after* my leg was broken.

The contract was ethically binding, you'd say. We had agreed in principle. Mr. Cooke had given his word that everything would be worked out. The legal fact remained, we had not signed the thing, and I was a 36-year-old quarterback in a hospital bed with my leg broken in two.

There in bed, the old broken-down quarterback realized, "The Redskins can walk away from this deal. They owe me nothing."

I prayed that wouldn't happen and had no reason to think it would, because Mr. Cooke's dealing with me had always been more than fair. My only complaint had been that he dragged it out, almost like he was playing a game with me. He enjoys power and he knew he had me by the short hairs. In 1985, when I wasn't playing well, I'd bug him every two or three weeks about getting the deal in writing. He'd say, "Look, you go out and play well the next couple of weeks, then we'll get it taken care of."

Maybe the unsettled contract bothered my play in '85. I don't know. But this is for sure: a signed contract would have made me feel a lot better.

The eventual terms of the contract were a two-year extension and a $1 million bonus going back to the last two years of the old contract. So my 1984 salary would be increased retroactively from $350,000 to $850,000. My '85 salary would go from $400,000 to $950,000. Then the '86 salary would be $1,050,000, and the '87 salary would be $1,150,000.

Mr. Cooke had those numbers written on the paper he showed me that day in his office. Nice numbers. Thank you, Mr. Cooke.

That day, a wiser man, I gave no interviews.

17
Paid to Talk

One day in training camp, I was approached by a reporter from ABC-TV who wanted to ask some questions, primarily questions related to the fact that I was older than most starters in the league. This was 1985, and I had begun to talk to the press again, but with restraint.

Well, it didn't take more than a minute to realize that this guy knew nothing about football. His first question was the tip-off: "Do you think your age is a factor?" Factor in what? I was 36. That's young. Next question.

"Some great quarterbacks have never won a Super Bowl. Frank Tarkenton never won one. What do you think about Frank Tarkenton's career?"

Frank Tarkenton? He is asking a professional football player about *Frank* Tarkenton? I was waiting for him to ask next how the center squats down and hatches all those little footballs.

I was insulted by his ignorance, and I told myself that if I ever ended up on the other side of the microphone, I was going to be a professional and do my homework.

So in 1986, when CBS gave me the opportunity to do just that, I learned an important lesson: boy, it's not as easy as it looks.

After all those years of answering the questions, the *same* questions, over and over again, it was a real challenge to come up with something new and refreshing. And it was an even greater challenge to be interviewing those very people who, until months before, had been solely responsible for my countless sleepless nights.

One of those I had a chance to talk with was the defensive coordinator of the Dallas Cowboys, Ernie Stautner. Over the years, I came to think of him as my enemy, probably because it was Ernie's job to make my life miserable on at least two Sundays every season. This was the man who told Randy White what to do to that hot dog Theismann. And it was my job to find weaknesses in Stautner's defense and exploit them.

So it was strange to find myself as a TV analyst sitting across a table from Ernie Stautner and asking him to tell me about the Cowboys' defensive plans. One look at Ernie Stautner and you say, "Now there's a football coach." He has a carved-in-granite face with a strong chin and eyes bright as fire. And the more we talked about our days as enemies, the more I liked Ernie.

I can't imagine a job that's more fun than playing in the National Football League. But now that I'm out of uniform and into the TV booth, I've learned one thing I never knew as a player. The NFL is full of great people, people who are open and honest and want to help you do your job. Heaven knows I need their help.

It would be a lie to say my work for CBS is as satisfying as my work on the field. I've never found any job that comes close to producing the adrenaline rush of competition under pressure. But I'd also be lying if I said commentating is a piece of cake. It's hard, and the more I do it, the more I respect men like Jack Buck, Pat Summerall, and John Madden. What John does with that "Telestrator"—drawing directional lines on the screen before a replay is run—may look easy, but you have five seconds to do it and you better be right. John is a virtuoso with that magic pen.

He is the absolute best in the business, because he gives so much life, fun, and knowledge to the fans. He's like a cartoon show: "Bang!" "Boom!" "Pop!" John's a big, jolly guy who just makes you feel good to see and hear him. He's Santa Claus doing color.

As a player, the game was life and death to me, and I took it very seriously. I try to approach my broadcast work with the same intensity. The bottom line is to help the TV viewer have fun. A color man can't be too technical; you're there to comment, not confuse. But you don't want to be so simplistic that you insult the fans' intelligence. Fans know a bad play when they see one, and you want the color commentator to confirm it. The idea is to tell the audience something it didn't know and tell it in a light, entertaining way—and do it in 13 seconds of air time, while the director counts down the seconds before cutting you off to go to a commercial.

I realize now that I could not have left football cold turkey. I never wanted to coach (what would I have done if I wound up with a player like *me*?). Thank goodness I didn't have to find out, because one day after being waived by the Redskins I signed with CBS. If I can't play the game, working football on TV is the next best thing, for two good reasons.

One, I loved to play football. Two, I loved to watch football. After a home game at one o'clock, I'd go to my restaurant and catch the second half of that day's doubleheaders. Monday nights and Thursday nights, I'd be watching football. I really am a fan.

In 1984, at a St. Louis roast for defensive tackle Dave Butz, I ran into Jack Buck and said, "I admire your work as a sportscaster, and if I'm lucky enough to get into broadcasting when I'm done playing ball, you're the man I'd love to work with." Jack has that touch of class that makes him special. I also thought his experience would help a rookie who would surely need it. As luck would have it, in 1986 I was Jack's partner.

My first season in the booth was fun, and our producer, Mike Burks, and director Larry Cavalina were great. After 32 years in the business, Jack shared his booth with a rookie, and not just any rookie, but one with a reputation. Jack, God love him, had everyone saying to him, "What in the world are you going to do to survive in that booth with Joe Theismann talking all the time? You'll never get a word in edgewise!"

OK, I have spoken a few sentences in my time, and if you add them up, maybe a few paragraphs. But the booth was Jack's home court, and if I started rambling, he would reach over, very kindly, and just squeeze my arm a little to tell me to slow down. Or during a commercial break, he'd say, "Let's take a play off and let the action speak for itself." A class act, Jack Buck.

The weekly regimen for an analyst is not unlike a quarterback's, as far as homework goes. I study the personnel on both teams and look at tapes of the teams' most recent games. On Thursday or Friday I try to interview the offensive and defensive coordinators; during the week and on Saturday I go to the practices. Some Saturdays, Mike Burks would run the tape of our last game to see how I could improve.

One thing I've learned from being up in the booth is that you can really see the receivers better up there than when you're running around behind the line. Those guys are *open*. And you can see if a defensive end is closing in on the quarterback. I'll be sitting there saying, "Look out!" to no one in particular. Defenses are a lot easier to read from up in the booth.

One of my concerns when I took the broadcasting job was how I'd be accepted by other players and coaches. Of all the coaches we interviewed in 1986, only Gene Stallings of St. Louis seemed initially wary. Not that he wasn't open with me, but it was Gene's first season as the Cardinal coach and he hadn't been through all the pregame TV interviews. After we finished talking, he said, "I sure hope none of what we've discussed gets to the other side."

No way that would ever happen. If it did, we'd be shut out of every coach's office in the league, and rightly so.

By the end of the season, we'd done seven Cardinal games, and I felt practically like a Cardinal quarterback. So I told him: "After four games, a guy is supposed to get full salary for making the team. How about it?"

One of the things I like about Gene, just as I had about Joe Gibbs, was that he knew football was a tough game. If you're going to win in the NFL, you've got to be tough, mentally and physically. He believed what Bear Bryant said: "It ain't playing football unless you put your nose where it ain't wanting to go."

Gene played for Bryant at Texas A & M in the '50s, and he tells this story about the time Bear took the team to some godforsaken camp out in the desert. Gene said: "We'd ride a bus along a cliff to the practice field, and most days I'd hope the bus would go off the cliff. I wasn't going to quit, but if the bus went off the cliff, that would be an honorable way out. We went to camp with two busloads of guys and by the end we only had half a busload left."

One Sunday, Bear walked in and said, "How many of you guys want to go to church?" Gene said everyone figured this was a chance to get out of another scorching practice, so up went the hands. Bear said: "Boys, I'm really proud of you. Church'll be great today. We'll go right after practice."

I was really excited and curious about my first chance to broadcast a Redskin game. How would the players react to me? Would they invite me to play cards? Would I accept? Should I accept? Will Joe Gibbs tell me what I need to know? How honest could I be if they played poorly? All these questions raced through my mind.

Once the game got started, it was just like old times. I watched coach Don Breaux signal in plays to the quarterback. I knew every play. So I began telling the TV audience what play was coming. "Now watch for Art Monk over the middle as the primary receiver," or, "Watch Russ Grimm and Joe Jacoby pull to their right on this play." I felt I had a chance to give the viewers a real opportunity to see inside the game.

I wasn't revealing any secrets that any NFL team couldn't figure out by watching films. Besides, Joe Gibbs is smarter than that. Coaches always protect their signal system by making slight changes, especially when the ex-quarterback in the booth helped invent the system.

The most difficult part of this rookie's TV work was Saturday interviews with players. On Saturdays, players just do not want to sit in the locker room and answer questions. It's supposed to be a short day. They can't say much, anyway, because they don't want to tip their hand or get the other team fired up.

So, knowing this firsthand, I still had to be bold and just walk up to the players and ask those questions. They always treated me cordially, but it's still going to take some time for me to become more a reporter and less a player, to put my old personal feelings aside. If I ever can.

Even as a player, I never hated the Cowboys the way some players are said to hate their primary rivals. You have too many other things to worry about without getting petty about things like that. I have a tremendous respect for what Tom Landry created in Dallas.

It was a thrill, then, to be a "reporter" going to see Coach Landry and having him be so open about his team. Same thing with Buddy Ryan at Philadelphia. Buddy has a master plan. He wants to sell tickets and he wants to win games. And winning is his number one priority.

Through all of my TV work in 1986, the single toughest coach to get anything from was Joe Gibbs. It is his personality to be guarded when talking about his football team. That was okay with me. I already knew what the Redskins would do.

Joe did tell me one thing I had wondered about for almost three years. We were comparing the 1986 team to the

Super Bowl teams of '82 and '83, and he brought up that screen pass against the Raiders in the Super Bowl. It was one of those things we hadn't really wanted to talk about, sort of like asking someone how their root canal went.

He said, "Joe, you know when you asked me if I was sure I wanted to call that play? I should have been suspicious right away."

We laughed together.

18
Yes, Dexter, the Cowboys Are Still in the League

I love my work in television, but there are those things I really miss about being a player. The Cowboys, for example.

Huh? He *misses* the Cowboys? Absolutely. Well, I don't miss the nightmares about Ernie Stautner's defense, but I do miss being part of that incredible rivalry, the fierce competition that grips two entire cities. There was nothing quite like that week before The Game—it was all anyone talked about and you couldn't escape it.

It wasn't hatred that motivated us as much as a mutual respect for talent and organization. Both teams wanted to be the best in the NFC East, and there's only room for one at the top.

As a player, you prepared for that game as you prepared for no other. This wasn't just another football game; it was a battle royale. Our meetings were a study in deception and concentration. Our practices reached new levels of intensity. Total preparedness, at any cost. For that week you might not speak to your wife or girlfriend, and she'd have to understand. This was Cowboy Week.

And if the practices and meetings weren't enough to contend with, there was the media, always finding a way to add to the hype. While we were trying not to tip our hand about a new secret weapon we might be planning to use, the media would be at every practice session trying to pick up on that one element that might be the difference in the game. Why is Monk limping? Why isn't Riggins practicing? Doesn't it look like the defense is having trouble against the pass? All those questions, all the vultures just waiting. We would try to stay out of the papers to keep from antagonizing anyone, but there was always someone who couldn't resist calling Roger Staubach a sissy to see if he'd get mad enough to blow his concentration.

If you couldn't get excited about playing the Cowboys, you probably weren't breathing. In the twelve years I played for the Redskins, the winner of those games was almost always assured a playoff spot. *That* was exciting. The plain and simple truth was that one of the teams was the best in the NFC East, and the other merely thought it was.

George Allen was the catalyst for a lot of the hype and hysteria that surrounded the rivalry. He'd post guards in any office building around Redskin Park that had a view of our practice field. He had his chief of security, Ed "Double O" Boynton, walk the perimeter of the practice field to be sure no one was spying. God love him, "Double O" had to be all of 5'9", 145 pounds. I have no idea what he would have done if he actually caught someone spying on us. But I'm sure he would have found a way to stop them. After all, this was war.

Even in our meetings, George would let us know how much he hated "those damn Cowboys." He'd say: "Those damn Cowboys, I can't stand them in those pretty, clean, shiny uniforms. When we get done with them, they won't be pretty, clean, *or* shiny. They don't like to be hit, they want to finesse us. Well, the way to beat them is to be physical, make them pay a price. Whenever the ballcarrier hits the hole, don't just tackle him—*punish him.* If the receiver is going out for a pass, make him pay a price. A big price."

When I first came to the Redskins, this was all sort of new to me, but it didn't take long to develop that special "hate" for the Cowboys. They were the "Goody-Two-Shoes" of the NFL, overrated because they had conned the media with their slick, shiny image, and we were a ragtag group of old men and unproven rookies, or so George Allen wanted us to believe. It was his way of motivating the Over-the-Hill-Gang.

After George was replaced in 1978 by Jack Pardee, the balance of power began to shift. Where we had once been equals, the Cowboys began to show signs of dominance. Under Pardee, a lot of the hype that had been so much a part of George Allen's technique had disappeared. Jack simply was not the communicator George was. He tried his best to charge us up with fire-and-brimstone speeches, but it just wasn't his nature. After a while, there were very few of us who remembered how to "hate those damn Cowboys." The older players were slowly being replaced, and the team was in transition. Cowboy Week had become a time to be pensive and hope we didn't do or say anything to get the Cowboys mad at us. Not that we didn't believe we could beat them, because we *did* believe and we *had* beat them, but the fact was, emotionally, our weaponry was limited.

Our first game against the Cowboys under Jack Pardee was a Monday night game, with the President of the United States in attendance. We had not stirred up any controversy all week. All we talked about in the press was how good the Cowboys were, what a great quarterback Roger was, and how Drew Pearson and Tony Hill were darn near unstoppable. The Cowboy defense was playing great, we said, with Randy White, Ed Jones, Harvey Martin, and Dee Dee Lewis all having great years. The compliments were flying. You'd have thought it was a first date, not a football game.

In those days, if I wasn't creating a problem with my mouth, trouble seemed to be just waiting out there for me to walk by. I had finally won the quarterback job from Billy Kilmer, and I felt like this was my first big start. I had

certainly started other games, but this was to me a true test
of whether I could really play with the big boys. I had never
doubted that I could, which was part of my problem, but
now I finally had a chance to prove it.

The game was a defensive battle, and with time running
out we were ahead 9–3. The Cowboys had called their last
timeout. We had the ball backed up deep in our own end.
The coaches didn't want to risk a handoff, so they told me
to take the snap, watch the clock, and step out of the end
zone when time ran out. We win, 9–5. Made sense to me.
Well, you know that saying, "The best-laid plans of mice
and men often go astray"? I was about to lead this one
astray.

I got into the huddle, called the play, and prepared to
pass my first big test as a pro quarterback. I took the snap,
concentrating on holding onto the ball—I didn't want to
fumble and ruin my big chance to be a hero. Once I got the
ball, I began running backward toward our end zone, just
as I was told. I watched the clock tick down . . . 4 . . . 3 . . .
2 . . . 1 . . . 0. Great, we had won, and I'm standing on the
field waving the ball in the air, full of the thrill of victory.
Only problem was, I had neglected to run out of the end
zone. I was still about three yards from the end line, which
meant the ball was still in play, and if a Cowboy pounced
on me and I fumbled, they would win, 10–9.

Of course, *they* realized this too, and proceeded to knock
the daylights out of me. But I didn't fumble, thank God.
Still, that wasn't the worst of it. The Cowboys were, shall
we say, annoyed at my gesture of waving the ball in the air
as the seconds ticked off the clock, and they interpreted my
actions as taunting. And the Dallas Cowboys did not
appreciate being "taunted" by an upstart quarterback who
was still wet behind the ears. A brawl nearly broke out, and
a lot of words were exchanged, most of them directed at me.
The message was clear: if they had their way, the next time
we met I was going to get my "ass kicked."

Well, to make a long story short (and a lot less painful),
they were right. In Texas Stadium on Thanksgiving Day,

they beat us soundly. And I came out of that game with a broken collarbone and two cracked ribs, compliments of Randy White and Ed Jones.

Year after year, our games were like that. In 1979 we lost our final meeting of the season 35–34 to Dallas in the game that made Roger Staubach a greater legend than he already was. He rallied his team from a 13-point deficit with only about two minutes to play. I believe it was the greatest game of his career.

The Redskins had reached the point where we were getting beaten consistently by "those damn Cowboys." The games *used* to be fun because they *used* to be between two evenly matched teams who *used* to be in the playoff picture. Used to be. Those days were gone. We lost both games in 1980, which, along with other things, prompted a coaching change.

At first, Joe Gibbs really didn't have a strong sense of the feelings between the Redskins and Cowboys. But it didn't take long for him to find out. Beating the Cowboys became a priority. But like Pardee before him, he didn't want anyone saying anything to the media that could in the slightest way irritate the Cowboys.

You see it happen all the time. A player makes some dumb remarks about the other team. Those remarks become headlines. The opponent takes the clippings from the newspapers and posts them in the locker room for everyone to ponder. So now they have not only the usual animosity but they have these clippings to constantly reinforce their dislike for the other team. This is common practice around the league, and to be honest, whenever I'd see a derogatory item about me or my teammates, it *did* put me in a different frame of mind. Before, I just wanted to beat them; now I wanted to beat them and make them eat every word, letter by letter.

After 1981, the balance of power began to swing back in our favor. Although we lost to Dallas once in 1982 (our only defeat that season), we could feel the stirrings of that old Redskin pride, the pride that goes with taking a

Cowboy scalp. It was in the NFC championship game that I really felt the emotion of this long-standing rivalry. We didn't just beat them, we crushed them, as they had done to us so many times before.

So began a period of total dominance by the Redskins. And it wasn't until three years later, on September 9, 1985 (my birthday), that I could feel that dominance slip a bit. They beat us in the season opener. No, let me rephrase that—they *humiliated* us in the season opener. I can't ever remember feeling any lower in my career (I threw five interceptions), and that includes our defeat in Super Bowl XVIII.

Did I really "hate" the Cowboys? Do players really hate each other as much as it seems? Honestly, I don't believe we hated each other in the literal sense of the word. Drew Pearson was a high school teammate of mine and a close friend, but if we were playing the Cowboys and Drew had his head knocked off, I wouldn't be the first in line to help him screw it back on. I would, however, be the first in line after the game to ask him how he felt.

It's not hate. It's a rivalry built on mutual respect and competition between two fine organizations. As for the ongoing battle between the two teams, I'll be watching to see which team is up to the task of challenging the Giants for the division title.

19
Outside the Huddle

Back when I was still playing football, a certain Redskin backup quarterback used to say to me, "How's it going, old man?" I'd look up and there'd be Jay Schroeder, grinning and saying, "Not a bad pass for a guy as old as you." This stuff never really bothered me because I knew he was only kidding (you *were* kidding, weren't you, Jay?), but I'll say this: he made me more determined than ever to keep that youngster right where he was, which was on the bench watching me work.

Unfortunately, my tibia and fibula had other ideas, and now I watch *him* work. And I have to say, I like what I see. In his first full season, he took his team to the NFC championship, he went to the Pro Bowl, and he didn't merely break some long-standing Redskin records, he shattered them. Jay is one of the most physically gifted quarterbacks I've seen. He has great poise, and no, I'm not going to add "for a young quarterback." A great athlete is a great athlete, and some people are just naturally poised. Jay is one of those people. He has a strong arm—not a Bradshaw gun, but close—and deceptive quickness. He has the ability to play right up there with Phil Simms and John Elway, who are the cream of the '80s crop, along with Joe Montana and Tommy Kramer.

When people aren't asking me what I think of Jay Schroeder, they're asking what I think of the current Redskin team. How do you think they're doing without you? Not a kind question, but a valid one. What does the team need to do to improve? How good is the defense?

The Redskins did very well without me, without John Riggins, without Mark Moseley. They did very well because, unlike many sports, football is dependent on teamwork. One guy can't pull it off. We'd all like to think we make a crucial difference, but the truth is, we don't. Some players can make a team exciting, like Joe Morris does for the Giants or Marcus Allen for the Raiders or as John Riggins did for the Redskins. But as far as being the whole show, it takes a lot more.

The 1986 Redskins were winners because they relied on a lot of people to win; they didn't have to lean on one or two players to carry the team. They had Schroeder throwing deep to Gary Clark or Art Monk, setting up the winning score, or maybe it was Darrell Green picking off a pass in the end zone to seal a victory. Or maybe George Rogers was plowing in from the two-yard line. They had the talent to beat you any number of ways.

But these Redskins didn't win like the Redskins I played with. Patience on offense was the hallmark of our Super Bowl teams, as was a physical toughness that enabled us to win games with Riggins's running. We were a run-first, pass-last team. If we had the lead late, or if we were within two points, we figured the game was ours because we'd just drive the ball down their throats until either the game was over or we were in position for Moseley to kick one.

That style of offense had been very effective, but in 1986, the Redskins moved away from it to an offense that used the long pass as the primary weapon. So, an old quarterback

might ask, what was going on? This new team didn't run
a controlled offense. They didn't dominate their opponents
like we did. They had developed their own style, a very
effective one, I might add, but not one that can win for you
consistently in the NFL.

One problem that faced Joe Gibbs was that he suddenly
had an abundance of offensive talent, and he had to adapt
his philosophies to fit the talent on hand. Joe looked
around and saw a young quarterback who could throw the
ball a mile. He saw four of the best receivers in football—
Art Monk, Gary Clark, Clint Didier, and Kelvin Bryant. So
as a coach, you look at all that talent and think to yourself,
"Hmmm, we'll throw the ball 45 times a game and light
up the scoreboards."

But wait, there's more! Gibbs also had one of the finest
offensive lines in the game. With Joe Jacoby at tackle and
Russ Grimm at guard, the Redskins had the best one-two
punch in the league. There are few better offensive tackles
than Jake. As for Grimm, he could be All-Pro at any
position in the line.

And then there was an outstanding running back in
George Rogers who is as good a back as there is in football
today. He's had one major problem, though, and that's
filling the shoes of another great back, Riggins. People will
never forget John's contribution to the team or his unique
style of play, and it's unfortunate that George can't be
judged on sheer ability. I know how he feels, because I
remember what it was like trying to step into the sneakers
of Sonny Jurgensen and Billy Kilmer.

But back to Joe Gibbs's dilemma. He has all that talent,
but only one football. So who does he give it to? I don't
believe he's figured it out yet, and I can't wait to see what he
does. My guess is that he and Bobby Beathard will do the
hard work necessary to regain a solid offensive balance. It's
not that far away. Maybe the Redskins of '86 weren't a Super
Bowl team, but they were 13-4 (the most victories since
1983), and they went to the playoffs and knocked off the

defending champion Chicago Bears—in Chicago yet. Losing then to the Giants, the eventual Super Bowl winners, was no embarrassment.

Then there's the Redskin defense. It seems to me that some of those guys are getting a little long in the tooth. Dave Butz is no spring chicken (although he's as strong as ever; you don't measure Dave's strength in pounds, you use buildings), and the linebackers—Rich Milot, Neal Olkewicz, and Monte Coleman, all a little balding—are reaching the twilight of their careers. The one glaring weakness in the defense is at cornerback. On one side you have the Darrell Green, for whom teams have tremendous respect. I sure did. Even in practice I didn't want to throw where he was. The guy was tough on your ego. You'd think your receiver was past him, and then, *boom,* Darrell would close the gap and either intercept the pass or knock it away.

But Darrell can play only one side. If the Redskins can get a quality cover guy to take some of the pressure off him, the entire defensive scheme will undoubtedly improve.

And then there's Dexter Manley. Defensive ends don't come much quicker than Dexter, nor do they come much stronger. They do, however, come quieter. (Ah, to be young again. To say what you want, to be free to be your own man . . . No, thank you.)

It might seem I'm knocking a successful team, but I'm not. I just believe that when Joe Gibbs lies awake at night imagining how his team should win, he's not imagining the scenario that emerged in 1986. He knows that you can't make it as a perennial contender if you live by the big pass. I think that if he can, he'll go back to the run-first, controlled passing offense. He won before with that strategy, and he can certainly do it again.

As for Jay Schroeder, I know he thinks of me as just an "old man," but the old man has a few ancient words of advice for him. Jay, forget about what you did in 1986. Don't try to be what you were. Get ready for each season as a new and wonderful learning experience. You're starting over again, and you'll be judged on what you accomplish today, not on what you did in the past.

Coach Gibbs told me recently that Jay is getting to be more like me every week. I am not sure what that means, but it might explain why Joe has so much more gray hair.

20
The Long Road Back

Jan. 20, 1986
   I visited Dr. Jackson today, and he removed my walking cast so I could walk around the office. Boy, did that feel great after two months. He is very pleased with my progress and so am I.
   I start therapy today and I get my walking brace (with the ugliest shoe in the world attached to the bottom).
   I'm trying to work the ankle loose so I can start walking normally.

The journal of my rehabilitation began with that entry full of relief and can-do enthusiasm. In my mind, there was no question about the future. Joe Theismann would play quarterback again in the National Football League. First, I would be walking normally, then jogging and running, then doing sprints and dashes on the football field. The only question was when.

March 2.
I walked with Cathy Lee for 1½ hours in the sand
in Florida.
March 3.
We walked another 1½ hours in the sand. The ankle
feels GREAT!!

The broken leg had changed everything. Not getting to
play those last five games of '85 made me realize how much
I wanted football. Wanted, not needed. It's the same thing
that got Joe Montana out of the hospital in '86. Joe had
back surgery and was playing again in two months. If that
amazed the doctors, it didn't surprise me at all. Joe was
young, he was in great shape, and the thought of never
playing again—it's frightening to think you'll never again
be the person you always were—was enough to turn up the
flame in him.

In *Rocky IV,* Apollo Creed comes back from retirement to
fight the Russian giant Ivan Drago. Everyone asks why the
champ would do it. He's got everything, money, fame,
security. "Because I'm a warrior," Apollo says, and this was
a war. It was his nature to fight. He could not *not* fight, just
like Sugar Ray Leonard coming back twice.

Quarterbacks feel the same stuff. On my rehab journal
there is pasted a sheet of paper with two words written in
red letters: "The Comeback."

April 23.
I ran for the first time today without having to take
anything for pain. I played three games of
racquetball with Bubba Tyer, and the only area of
soreness in my leg was on the shin above the break
and in the ankle on both sides.
April 26.
The ankle is beginning to loosen up, but I am still
having trouble walking with weight on my big toe.
May 2.
I went to Redskin Park to throw and to run on the

treadmill. Trying to get in shape and have my leg take some pounding.

May 5.

Worked out, threw, ran for seven minutes. Still a lot of soreness above the break. Leg hurt for two hours after the workout.

May 9.

Worked out at the Park. Ran 15 minutes at 6 mph, lifted and threw. Today my left knee is really starting to bother me. The range of motion in my ankle seems to have leveled out. Trying to throw today was the toughest time I had. I can't dash or sprint out without having pain in the ankle. And when I set up to throw, the ankle and leg feel weak.

Baseball pitchers and quarterbacks know the arm is only part of the deal. Power comes from your legs. Without the proper balance and support, the arm often isn't strong enough to do what's necessary.

For a right-handed thrower, the right leg is the set leg. You push off that leg. And that's the leg I broke. Without strength there, I had to compensate in my arm. Such is the path to a sore arm, even a dead arm. The great pitcher Dizzy Dean was never the same after trying to pitch on a foot injured by a line drive. He favored the foot, which put unusual strain on his arm.

May 14.

Today I took my physical. Dr. Charlie Jackson took another X-ray, and I really am disappointed.

The outside part of my leg has remolded great, but the other side is just not responding as well. Dr. Jackson said it doesn't look good for playing again.

I will continue to work, and we are now going to try a stimulator to aid in bone growth.

May 17.

It is Saturday. I will just do some more walking to try to get the inside part of my foot to come down

on the ground. The foot looks like a cupped hand. I
can walk only on the outside portion. My big toe
seems permanently lifted off the ground.

May 24.
Cathy Lee has come home, and we worked hard.
She gave me a jump rope to add to my exercise
routine. Three to five minutes of jumping rope with
a three-pound rubber rope is not my idea of fun.
 As I walk and run backward at the farm, Cathy
Lee chases me. I want her to catch me, but she
makes believe she is Lawrence Taylor and speeds up
and slows down when I do. Finally she catches me,
and I enjoy the agony of defeat.

Another by-product of a broken leg is that the bone often
heals shorter than it used to be. Right now, if I lean on my
left leg, I'm six feet tall. On my right leg, I'm five–eleven.
Because the one leg is shorter, my back is now out of whack.
 After my first few times back at Redskin Park trying to
throw, everything was sore. My leg, my ankle, my back, my
arm. I'd had sore arms, but never like this. This was deep
in the muscle. It was an entirely new pain being caused by
the imbalance in my delivery.

June 1.
This was not a happy day. I had to do an
appearance in Norfolk, Virginia, at the Leigh
Memorial Hospital, where I had lunch with a
number of orthopedic surgeons. They looked at my
leg. I'm not good at names, but I remember a Dr.
Johnson because he is the first person I met who
thought all the TV replays of me breaking my leg
were "neat."
 Dr. Johnson and another surgeon examined the leg
and took an X-ray. They both said DO NOT PLAY
racquetball or tennis. They said the tibia is only
half healed and I could easily break the bone again

by pivoting on it. They said it would be at least a
year before I would be able to try to play football.
They said I could play golf, nothing else.

Today is the first time since I was hurt that I am in
serious doubt about being able to play ball again.

It is one lousy feeling.

June 6.

Our golf outing in Memphis was canceled because
of rain. I did meet Dr. George Coors. Dr. Coors
mentioned that with blood flow to that area of my
leg diminished, if I break the leg again I could lose
the leg.

June 10.

Got a treatment at UCLA. Worked with towel and
manual rotation of ankle with resistance 25 times.
The leg is still weak and I still can't run and the
whole thing sucks. I constantly keep asking myself
why the hell I am doing this. I can't play
racquetball, can't play tennis, and, believe me, golf
can't fill the void I feel.

That fire inside me has got me confused. I feel
great, but I just can't do my thing. It's driving me
nuts.

June 26.

Frustration. It just doesn't seem to be getting better.

June 27.

Saw Dr. Jackson today. X-rays show the inside
portion of the bone is not healing properly. What a
bummer.

July 8.

More upsetting information. Dr. Robert Kerlan in
L.A. is one of the best in dealing with sports
injuries. He suggested that I won't be able to play
again. He also said no tennis, no racquetball. Not
even golf for the time being.

I think it's time to start thinking about life after
football.

On July 25, after failing my preseason physical examination, I went to Mr. Cooke's house to talk about ending my career with the Redskins. He wasn't certain whether I would retire or ask to be waived, so he had prepared two press releases. Not that there was much difference; being waived at age 36 with a broken leg not yet healed is effectively retirement.

It was my contention that I was going to be OK again and didn't need to announce any retirement. The word "retirement" seemed so final, and I wasn't ready emotionally to accept that. To retire would be to admit defeat and say, "Yes, it's done, it's over."

Cathy Lee and I drove out to Mr. Cooke's farm. We had a very warm meeting during which I insisted on being waived instead of retiring. With Cathy Lee's encouragement, Mr. Cooke put away the official news release already drawn up, and in its place he wrote a personal letter of thanks to me. He also used it as the media announcement of the waiver.

Dear Joe:
For 12 years now, since February 22, 1974, when you joined the Redskins from the Canadian Football League, you have performed admirably in every role.
Think of it:
1. Philadelphia Maxwell Club Bert Bell Award as NFL Player of the Year for the 1982 season.
2. NFL Most Valuable Player for 1983 season.
3. Pro Bowl for both 1982 and 1983 seasons.
4. Most Valuable Player for the 1983 Pro Bowl.
5. NFL Miller Man of the Year award for the 1982 season for the entire League. (Award given to people who contribute generously of time and effort off the field to their communities.)
6. Hold 8 Redskin club records.
7. Played in 163 consecutive games (third longest streak in Redskin history).

8. Above all, you've quarterbacked the Redskins to two Super Bowls.

On the field, you never let down. You were always up, up, up; undeniably cocky, gutsy, and one of those rare guys whose reach exceeded his grasp, bringing the "heaven" he sought.

Now we come to the end of your playing marathon. What a marvelously productive run it has been. To Redskins fans, to the club, and to me personally, your record bears proof of your sterling accomplishments. They'll be hard to beat, Joe.

Since your doctors tell me that your leg has not mended properly, that you should not play again, I have urged you to retire. In your usual few thousand words, you say no. By straining somewhat I catch a glimmering of what you're driving at. But only a glimmering. You refuse to be dissuaded from the only alternative to retirement, namely, you insist on being put on waivers.

You've made the decision. You're pleased with it, you say, and I am, well, only sort of pleased. To me, retirement is the right route, but you've cast your die for this waiver. So, considering the enormously pleasant, profitable, and winning career you, the Redskins, and I have enjoyed together, I give in to your wish.

What more can I say? Other than that your waiver request will be completed in accordance with the National Football League's Constitution and Bylaws Article XVIII (entitled "Waivers"). At least the waiver is one of the friendliest ever reached between an owner and a player; and for all I know, perhaps the *only* friendly one on record.

Joe, may good health, good luck, and all deserved success be yours. Joining me in expressing best wishes to you is Bobby Beathard, who says, "I'm satisfied that Super Bowl XVII and Super Bowl XVIII would not have been possible without you at the helm. We, all of us, thank you for these unique successes. Good luck, Joe."

Joe Gibbs adds, "We will miss you greatly. You have always demonstrated a high quality of style and timing. You have proved your greatness on the playing field. We wish you luck in all your future endeavors."

Joining Bobby Beathard, Joe Gibbs, and me in these sentiments are my son John and the entire Redskins organization.

Again, Joe, my warmest best wishes for the kind of success which will inevitably be yours in whatever field you choose.

Fond regards to you and Cathy Lee.

(Signed) Jack Kent Cooke

Every athlete, maybe every person, thinks he'll be a kid forever. You think the good times are never going to end. Intellectually, you know how foolish that thought is. But the brain, like the body, protects itself. In a perverse way, you need to think the fun is going to last forever. Otherwise, you risk being so frightened by the possibility of failure that you freeze up and you fail. So you lie to yourself: you say this is wonderful and I'm a great athlete and I'll play until I'm older than Kilmer and Jurgensen put together.

Then, just about the time you begin to believe your sweet lie, there comes the inevitable day of truth. The owner is asking you if you want to retire or be waived.

That night, I cried.

Aug. 10.

The Redskins play their first exhibition game today in Foxboro, Massachusetts, against New England. I didn't sleep well last night, probably because I'm a creature of habit and I was having my own pregame jitters.

We just finished 2½ hours of digging fence-post holes. Counts as weight lifting.

Sept. 3.
Treatment at Redskin Park. They have a new tub to
run in and it is great.
Oct. 8.
Worked out at the farm. Walked two miles. Lifted
in the garage.

I couldn't let go of the game. It had been the driving force
of my life for 20 years. Screw the doctors. I could play again.
The harder I worked out, the more convinced I was there
was a way to play again. I called Chuck Knox at Seattle and
Dan Henning at Atlanta. Both teams could have used a
quarterback with Super Bowl experience. Both coaches
were men I respected and would like to play for. Neither
one, I must admit, leaped for joy when I called; neither
asked me to come in for a workout. But that was OK. Just
calling them and talking about football brought a little
light into the dark hole of a depression unlike anything I'd
ever known.

I hated going to Redskin Park for treatments and workouts. After all those years of wanting nothing but to be a
Redskin, I absolutely hated going there.

It was like going into a house where you used to live.
Only now you don't recognize anybody. It was cold and
empty and lonely. I had been a part of that place, but now
I was a stranger there. Everything looked different, everything felt different. To have been so close and now to be so
far away hurt me.

There was no slow change to it, no chance to become
adjusted to the idea, no letting the memories gracefully fade
away. Bang, you're dead. Now you're here, now you're gone.
History.

Although everyone at Redskin Park was still nice to me,
it wasn't comfortable. The locker room had become an
alien place filled with bright, fresh, young faces. Who were
they? I was a stranger in the house I had loved.

The truth wiggled its way into my mind. The season had started and I was not even close to being able to play. I'd go run, only to find out I couldn't really run. It was as if my right leg wouldn't cooperate. Every time my foot hit the ground, it was ker-lump, ker-lump. No spring at all. Just dead weight. And if I didn't have explosion off that leg, I couldn't play quarterback. The ability to escape the sack was always one of my fortes. Without that mobility, I'd be a sitting duck, liable to be reinjured the first time anyone took a shot at me.

As hard as I had worked to get back, I had no power in that leg. I couldn't run properly. Nor could I set up on the leg and push off to throw. Most of this was the result of trauma transferred from my leg to the ankle during the injury. With the ankle messed up, I lost the full range of motion in my foot. The foot could move the full range up, but I couldn't push it all the way down, and so I couldn't exercise the full range of the muscles to build them up.

The healing of my tibia and fibula wasn't perfect, either. It left my leg with a slight bow that threw everything out of kilter. Most people can press all their toes against the floor. I can't. My right foot is cocked in such a way that the big toe is always off the ground. Any athlete will tell you that his big toe is critical to balance and strength. Mine was gone.

Oct. 28.
Worked out and threw. Leg and ankle really sore.
Oct. 29.
Threw and ran. Hurt big time.
Nov. 1.
Threw at Park and got treatment. Back is now sore.
Nov. 4.
Back is very sore and can't move.
Nov. 6.
Saw Dr. Jackson. Says no way can I play.

Out of habit one day, I started to walk to my locker. A player's locker is his second home. He suits up there, he stores his stuff, he eats lunch there. Guys put up pictures of their girlfriends or their wives and kids. They stack mail there. No trespassers allowed. This is his turf, his place.

The week I was hurt, they gave my locker to the new quarterback in town, Steve Bartkowski. In the summer of '86 they gave it to the latest new quarterback, Doug Williams.

No sooner had the vacancy sign gone up, the locker was filled. Twelve years for me in that spot, gone in a week.

The locker is not only someone else's now, he may have filled it with more pads and shoes than you had. It doesn't even look like your locker. You're getting the idea by now. Whether you like it or not, your career is over. You get the feeling that you just don't belong there.

They try to be nice. They say, "How're you doing?" "See you later, Joe." "Keep after it." But you know they have no idea what you're feeling. They can't know how much it hurts to be passing through, to not be part of it any longer. I'd done the same thing to other players. You just don't know how a guy feels on the way out until you're the guy.

I did it to Larry Brown, one of the greatest Redskins ever. He'd be coming in the locker room and I had no idea what he was feeling, how uncomfortable it must have been for him to walk around in there.

Not only Larry, very few guys who have played here can stay in that locker room more than five minutes. They can't stand the hurt, so they get out in a hurry. It never dawned on me why they'd be in such a hurry. Now I know. They were a vital part of the team and they felt alive. Suddenly, they are on the outside looking in, and they know it can never be the same again.

This game has so much beauty and so much pain. There are moments you wish you could preserve forever. Not many people ever experience such great highs. But then it's over. It just ends. Bang. The curtain falls. All is quiet and all is dark.

The team will get another quarterback. They'll break

your old records. They'll go on winning. And that's good.
I had my moments. As Mr. Cooke suggested in his letter, I
touched the poet's heaven. It's time to move on. It's time to
win in another way.

Nov. 7.
Leave for San Francisco. Working TV.

Postscript

The boy had a dream and he lived the dream. And in the living of the dream, he learned a lesson in reality. I learned that no one does it alone. So many people took the time to help me; not only to make me a better athlete, but also a better person.

Like many precocious athletes, I directed every day of my life to my game. No that there is anything wrong with dedication and sacrifice; given a second chance, I would spend just as much energy at making Joe Theismann the best quarterback he could be. Many times, though, I wished I'd paid more attention to making Joe Theismann a better guy.

It took a broken leg to end my playing days, and maybe it took the end of my playing days to teach me what life is all about. It's about love and caring. It's about sharing yourself with the ones who need you. Someone told me, "Friends multiply the joy and divide the sorrow." To my parents, to Cathy Lee, to all my friends, coaches and teammates who have long known what I only now am learning, thank you. Thank you very much for helping. It's my turn to give to you.